Paul Pry [a comedy in three acts]

John Poole

PAUL PRY.

A COMEDY, IN THREE ACTS.—BY JOHN POOLE.

Dramatis Personæ.

[See page 12.

As first performed at the Theatre Royal, Haymarket, on September 13th, 1825.

COLONEL HARDY	Mr. W. Farren.	GRASP (Steward to Witherton)	Mr. Younger.
FRANK HARDY	Mr. Raymond.	DOUBLEDOT (an Innkeeper) ...	Mr. C. Jones.
WITHERTON (an old Bachelor)...	Mr. Pope.	SIMON	Mr. Ross.
WILLIS (his Nephew, disguised		SERVANT	Mr. Jones.
as Somers)	Mr. W. Johnson.	ELIZA	Miss P. Glover.
STANLEY	Mr. Duff.	MARIAN	Miss A. Jones.
HARRY STANLEY (his Son)...	Mrs. Waylett.	MRS. SUBTLE...	Mrs. Glover.
PAUL PRY	Mr. Liston.	PHŒBE	Madame Vestris

Time of Representation, Two Hours-and-a-half.

No. 321. Dicks' Standard Plays.

COSTUME.

The Costume of Paul Pry, like that of many of the old Comedies, is generally incongruous, Colonel Hardy appearing in an old-fashioned Military Dress, and the other characters in fashionable modern costume. Much reform is necessary in this respect in all our Theatres.—EDITOR.

COLONEL HARDY.—Blue frock coat, buff waistcoat, white trousers.

FRANK HARDY.—Travelling costume.

WITHERTON.—Brown body coat, white waistcoat, drab breeches and gaiters.

WILLIS.—Modern suit.

STANLEY.—Dark frock coat, light waistcoat, dark trousers, boots.

HARRY STANLEY.—Modern suit.

PAUL PRY.—Body coat, striped waistcoat, and full striped trousers, tucked into high boots, double eye-glass, white broad-brimmed hat, turned up at the sides.

GRASP.—Dark suit, white cravat.

DOUBLEDOT.—Modern suit.

SIMON.—Livery.

ELIZA.—Elegant lady's dress.

MARIAN.—Neat merino dress.

MRS. SUBTLE.—Plain silk, apron, and cap.

PHEBE.—Neat dress of a lady's maid.

STAGE DIRECTIONS.

EXITS AND ENTRANCES.—R. means *Right*; L. *Left*; D. F. *Door in Flat*; R. D. *Right Door*; L. D. *Left Door*; S. E. *Second Entrance*; U. E. *Upper Entrance*; M. D. *Middle Door*; L. U. E. *Left Upper Entrance*; R. U. E. *Right Upper Entrance*; L. S. E. *Left Second Entrance*; P. S. *Prompt Side*; O. P. *Opposite Prompt.*

RELATIVE POSITIONS.—R. means *Right*; L. *Left*; C. *Centre*; R. C. *Right of Centre*; L. C. *Left of Centre.*

R.	RC.	C.	LC.	L.

** *The Reader is supposed to be on the Stage, facing the Audience.*

PAUL PRY.

ACT I.

SCENE I.—*A Village Inn. Table, two chairs, jug with ale, and two glasses.* DOUBLEDOT, R., *and* SIMON, L., *discovered drinking.*

Sim. Well, really, I must go, Mr. Doubledot, it will be a busy day at our house; master expects company to dinner.

Dou. Come, we must finish the mug; and when is Miss Eliza's wedding to take place?

Sim. Can't say; my master, Colonel Hardy, never lets anyone into his secrets.

Dou. Well, Miss Eliza's a nice young lady.

Sim. Ay, that she is; but she is a sly one. She looks as if butter wouldn't melt in her mouth; but she's a sly one, I tell you.

Dou. What makes you think that, Simon?

Sim. I don't mean any harm of her, for she's as kind a soul, bless her, as ever lived; but by putting this and that together, you know, we in the kitchen often know what is going on in the parlour better than the parlour folks themselves. She's in love.

Dou. That's natural enough, since she's going to be married.

Sim. But as she never saw the man she is to marry—

Dou. Sensibly argued; with whom, then?

Sim. We can't make that out. You know what a strict hand the Colonel is—passionate—severe—no one in his house dare say their soul is their own; so that, if our young lady were in love with twenty men, she would never dare tell her father of it. No, no, my master is not like his neighbour, old Mr. Witherton, who is led by the nose by a steward and a housekeeper.

Dou. Ah! poor old gentleman; but don't you think your young lady's maid, Miss Phebe, is in the secret?

Sim. May be, but she's as close-tongued as her mistress; besides, she never mixes with us. Miss Phebe's a devilish nice girl, Doubledot; here's wishing her a good husband, and she may have me for asking. (*Rises.*) Well, I must go, else I shall get chattering on the affairs of the family—a thing I never do. (*Comes forward,* L.) Ha! here comes Mr. Paul Pry.

Dou. Plague take Mr. Paul Pry. He is one of those idle, meddling fellows, who, having no employment themselves, are perpetually interfering in other people's affairs.

Sim. Ay, and he's inquisitive into all matters, great or small.

Dou. Inquisitive! why, he makes no scruple to question you respecting your most private concerns. Then he will weary you to death with a long story about a cramp in his leg, or the loss of a sleeve-button, or some such idle matter, and so he passes his days, "dropping in," as he calls it, from house to house at the most unseasonable times, to the annoyance of every family in the village. But I'll soon get rid of him.

Enter PAUL PRY, L.

Pry. Ha! how d'ye do, Mr. Doubledot?
(*Crosses to* C.)

Dou. Very busy, Mr. Pry, and have scarcely time to say "pretty well," thank ye.
(*Retires up,* R.)

Pry. Ha, Simon! you here. Rather early in the morning to be in a public house—sent here with a message from your master, perhaps. I say, Simon, when this wedding takes place, I suppose your master will put you all into new liveries, eh?

Sim. Can't say, sir.

Pry. Well, I think he might. Between ourselves, Simon, it won't be before you want 'em, eh?

Sim. That's master's business, sir, and neither yours nor mine.

Pry. Mr. Simon, behave yourself, or I shall complain of you to the Colonel. *Apropos*, Simon, that's an uncommon fine leg of mutton the butcher has just sent to your house—it weighs thirteen pounds five ounces.

Dou. (R.) And how do you know that?

Pry. I asked the butcher. I say, Simon, is it for roasting or boiling?

Sim. (L.) Half and half, with the chill taken off. There's your answer.

[*Exit Simon,* L.

Pry. That's an uncommon ill-behaved servant. Well, since you say you are busy, I won't interrupt you; only as I was passing, I thought I might as well drop in.

Dou. (R.) Then now you may drop out again. The London coach will be here presently, and——

Pry. No passengers by it to-day, for I have been to the hill to look for it.

Dou. Did you expect anyone by it, that you were so anxious?

Pry. No, but I make it my business to see the coach come in every day; I can't bear to be idle.

Dou. Useful occupation, truly.

Pry. Always see it go out—have done these ten years.

Dou. (*Going up.*) Tiresome blockhead! Well, good morning to you.

Pry. Good morning, Mr. Doubledot, you don't appear to be very full here.

Dou. No, no.

Pry. Ha! you are at a heavy rent. (*Pauses for an answer after each question.*) I've often thought of that—no supporting such an establishment without a deal of custom—if it's not asking an impertinent question, don't you find it rather a hard matter to make both ends meet when Christmas comes?

Dou. If it isn't asking an impertinent question, what's that to you?

Pry. Oh, nothing; only some folks have the luck

of it; they have just taken in a nobleman's family at the Green Dragon?

Dou. What's that—a nobleman at the Green, Dragon?

Pry. Travelling carriage and four. Three servants on the dickey and an outrider, all in blue liveries. They dine and stop all night; a pretty bill there will be to-morrow, for the servants are not on board wages.

Dou. Plague take the Green Dragon! How did you discover that they are not on board wages?

Pry. I was curious to know, and asked one of them. You know I never miss anything for want of asking; 'tis no fault of mine the nabob is not here.

Dou. Why, what had you to do with it?

Pry. You know I never forget my friends. I stopt the carriage as it was coming down the hill —stopt it dead, and said that his lordship—I took him for a lord at first—that, if his lordship intended to make any stay, he couldn't do better than go to Doubledot's.

Dou. Well?

Pry. Well, would you believe it?—out pops a saffron-coloured face from the carriage window, and says, "You're an impudent rascal for stopping my carriage, and I'll not go there if another inn is to be found within ten miles of it?

Dou. There! that comes of your confounded meddling. If you had not interfered, I should have stood an equal chance with the Green Dragon.

Pry. I'm very sorry, but I did it for the best.

Dou. Did it for the best indeed! Deuce take you. By your officious attempts to serve, you do more mischief in the neighbourhood than the exciseman, the apothecary, and the attorney, all together.

Pry. Well, there's gratitude! Now, really, I must go—good morning.

[*Exit Paul Pry, L.*

Dou. I've got rid of him at last, thank heaven!

Re-enter PAUL PRY, L.

Well, what now?

Pry. I've dropt one of my gloves.

Dou. You have not dropped it here.

Pry. Well, I didn't say I did drop it on that spot, but I have dropped it, and I suppose I may look for it. Well, that's very odd: here it is in my hand all the time.

Dou. Go to the devil!

[*Exit, R.*

Pry. Come, that's civil (*looking out*). Eh! there's the postman. I wonder whether the Perkinses have got letters again to-day? They have had letters every day this week, and I can't, for the life of me, think what they can—(*feels hastily in his pocket*). Apropos—talking of letters, here's one I took from him last week, for the Colonel's daughter, Miss Eliza, and I have always forgotten to give it to her; I dare say it is not of such importance (*peeps into it*). "Likely—unexpected—affectionate." I can't make it out. No matter, I'll contrive to take it to the house; by-the-bye though, I have a deal to do to-day—buy an ounce of snuff; fetch my umbrella, which I left to be mended; drop in at old Mr. Witherton's, and ask how his tooth is. I have often thought that if that tooth was mine, I'd have it out.

[*Exit, L.*

SCENE II.—*A Chamber at Witherton's. Table and chairs.*

Enter MRS. SUBTLE *and* GRASP, R.

Mrs. S. Don't threaten me, Mr. Grasp, for you know you are at least as much in my power as I am in yours, and that the exposure of either of us must be fatal to both.

Gra. Well, well, Mrs. Subtle, you must allow for the warmth of my temper.

Mrs. S. Your temper will one day bring down ruin upon us. We have sufficient control over Mr. Witherton to serve our every purpose; but by making him feel his subjection, by drawing the cord too tight, as you do, you run the risk of exciting his suspicions, and rousing him to rebellion.

Gra. Never fear; we have the Old Baby in leading strings, and may do with him just what we please.

Mrs. S. We might whilst he remained at his own place, in Wiltshire, away from all the world; but since his old friend, Colonel Hardy, has induced him to pass a few months here near him, a new influence has arisen.

Gra. And for that reason we must be the more rigid in the maintenance of our own. Then there's that young fellow, Willis, whom the Colonel has contrived to foist into his family; but I'll soon get rid of him.

Mrs. S. It is not Willis I fear, but the girl Marian. When we were at home, no one presumed to interfere in the arrangements of the household —that was our province; but here, however, I have taken a dislike to that girl, and she shall quit the house, displease whomsoever it may.

Gra. Indeed! it would displease me for one, and she shall remain.

Mrs. S. Shall! another such a word—Mr. Grasp, and——

Gra. So now, Mrs. Subtle, you would threaten me. Who was the inventor of all the calumnies which have for ever poisoned the mind of Mr. Witherton against his nephew, poor young Somers? By whose arts have they been prevented meeting each other? Who falsified some of the poor lad's letters—intercepted and suppressed others—impugned the character of the woman he chose for his wife.

Mrs. S. Who was it that—employed to forward the letters written to him by his uncle—destroyed them!—who for these three years has robbed, pillaged, plundered?

Gra. Both you and I!—Harkee, Mrs. Subtle, we have neither of us anything to gain by quarrelling. Give me your hand—there!

Mrs. S. (*Aside.*) The hateful wretch!

Gra. And now turn to a pleasanter subject.

Mrs. S. What subject?

Gra. One upon which I have been constant these five years—love. It relieves my heart, after a little misunderstanding between us, to say a tender word to you.

Mrs. S. Really, Mr. Grasp, your gallantry——

Gra. I was never wanting in gallantry towards the fair sex—so, once for all, my dear Mrs. Subtle, you and I are so confoundedly in dread of each other, the sooner we marry and make our interests one, the better.

Mrs. S. (*Aside.*) I'd sooner die. But you are so impatient.

Gra. Pooh, pooh, you have been shillyshallying

these five years; and it is time you should make up your mind that we unite our interests, play the same game, and have the old fellow more completely in our power; besides, there is no real happiness in a single life. Look at our master, or rather our slave; he is an old bachelor, and, with all his fortune, he is an unhappy man.

Mrs. S. (*Sighs.*) True, but I have once already been married, and——

Gra. Ay, but that was a marriage contracted contrary to your inclinations—our cause is different. You'll find me a tender indulgent husband; so I'll allow you till to-morrow to consider of my proposal, and then if you don't, hang me but I'll expose—but here comes the baby and Colonel Hardy, and that eternal Willis along with him. (*Crossing to L.*) Remember, my darling Mrs. Subtle (*shakes her hand*) to-morrow you consent to our making each other happy for life, or I'll trounce you.

[*Exit L.*

Mrs. S. I am indeed in his power; for in one moment he could destroy the fruits of ten long years of labour. To-morrow!—then I must bring Witherton to a decison to-day. My control over his affections is, I think—nay I'm sure—it is entire. The result cannot but be favourable, and once mistress here I will turn you to the dogs.

(*Retires up, R.*)

Enter WITHERTON, HARDY *and* WILLIS, S. E. R.

Har. You'll consider of it—what do you mean by considering of it? What is there to consider? Can't you say at once whether you will dine with me or not?

Wit. (L.) Not so loud, my dear friend, you agitate me.

Har. Then why the devil don't you make up your mind?—I hate the man who doesn't make up his mind. Do as I do—always make up your mind, right or wrong.

Wit. Well, well.

Har. Perhaps Mrs. Subtle, your housekeeper, won't give you leave. I say, Mrs. Subtle, is it you who refuse your master's leave to dine with me to-day?

Mrs. S. I, sir! Mr. Witherton is perfectly at liberty to do what he pleases.

Har. There, you are at liberty to do as you please; and so you ought to be. I shall expect you then—you have but to cross the garden to my house; so the walk won't fatigue you. You'll meet a friend or two—shan't tell you who, till you come—never do—and I shall have something to say to you, relative to my daughters Eliza's marriage—d'ye hear?

Wit. I do, my friend; and I should hear quite as well, though you did not speak so loud.

Har. And bring Willis with you, he is a good lad; I have a great respect for him, else I should not have recommended him to you. You are pleased with him, ain't you?

Wit. I am, indeed. Each day of the few months he has been a companion to me he has grown in my esteem: his good sense, his kindly disposition, his urbanity, have won from me the confidence and affection of a friend.

Har. That's well; and Marian—she doesn't disgrace my recommendation, I'll answer for it. Where is she?

Mrs. S. She's engaged in my room, sir. Mr.

Witherton received her into the family at your request; but really, I—I have so little to do, that an assistant is quite needless to me; and as I am for sparing my good master all the expense I can in the management of his house, it strikes me that——

Har. I think I could show him where one might be saved——

Wit. No matter. The expense is trifling, and the poor thing appears to be happy to be here; and Heaven knows that the sight of a happy face is the only solace in my lonely existence.

Har. Serve you right, you old fool, for not marrying in your youth; I don't wish to say anything unpleasant, but it serves you right, I tell you. And then to make matters worse you must needs go and pass your days at a melancholy place in Wiltshire, where you have only those about you, who—ah—as to your neglecting your nephew, I shall say nothing about that now, because I won't make you uncomfortable; but you'll repent it, I know you do; and you'll repent it more every day you live.

Wit. That is a subject I must not hear mentioned even by you.

Har. Why, now, who the deuce does mention it? Don't I this very moment say I won't mention it for fear of making you uncomfortable? Ah, you are a foolish old fellow—mark my words—you are a very foolish old fellow. (*Witherton crosses to L.*) I'll go home and talk to my daughter about marriage—bless her dear innocent little heart; there she is, I'll answer for it, quietly seated in the library, reading the *Spectator*, or painting daffodils on velvet. Well, good morning! I shall expect you! (*Shakes Witherton's hand violently.*)

Wit. I'll come, but—consider my nerves.

(*Goes up and sits, R.*)

Har. Plague take your nerves! but it serves you right—if you had lived a jolly life, as I have done, you would never have had any nerves. Good morning, Mrs. Subtle.

Mrs. S. I wish you a very good morning, sir; allow me to conduct you to the door.

Har. Willis, you will be sure to come with Mr. Witherton. (*Aside to him.*) The train is fairly laid: do you and your little wife be on your guard; and if we don't blow your enemies into the air—(*Muttering to Mrs. Subtle, who advances, L., and curtseys ceremoniously.*) Ah! confound you!

[*Exit Hardy and Mrs. Subtle, L.*

Wit. There goes a happy man. Oh, Hardy is right, I ought to have married in my youth.

(*Comes down, R.*)

Wil. (L.) And why did you not, sir?

Wit. With the fool's reason; I was unwilling to sacrifice my liberty. And what is the boasted liberty of a bachelor? He makes a solitary journey through life, loving no one, by none beloved; and when he reaches the confines of old age, that, which with a tender companion at his side, might have been to him a garden of repose, he finds a barren wilderness.

Wil. True, sir; and often with the sacrifice of his dear liberty into the bargain: avoiding the dreaded control of a wife, he dooms himself a slave to cunning and interested dependants.

Wit. (*Looking cautiously about.*) Willis, Willis, that I sometimes fear is my case; not that I have any reason to doubt the fidelity and attachment of Grasp or Mrs. Subtle, but they frequently assume an authority over me, which, however it may displease me, yet from a long lazy habit of submission I have scarcely the courage to resist.

Wil. (*Aside.*) My poor uncle!

Wit. But Mrs. Subtle is a good soul, a kind soul, and as attentive and affectionate towards me as a sister. Do you know that notwithstanding her humble situation here, she is well born, as she tells me, well educated, ay, and a very fine woman, too.

Wil. (*Aside.*) It is not difficult to see where this will end. You—you had a sister, sir.

Wit. I had; the mother of my ungrateful and disobedient nephew. She went abroad, died, and left an only son, this Edward Somers. He might have been a joy and comfort to me, he is my bane and curse! But let us speak of him no more: his very name is hateful to me.

Wil. This is the first time I ever ventured, sir. Duty and respect, which hitherto have constrained me to be silent, now bid me speak. What proofs have you of his ingratitude and disobedience?

Wit. The proofs are in this conduct. At his mother's death I wrote to him to come to England, told him of my intention to settle the bulk of my fortune upon him, to receive and consider him as my son, to—

Wil. You wrote to him?

Wit. Ay, and often; as Grasp and Mrs. Subtle can testify, for they saw my letters; but he neglected my commands—nay, did not even deign to notice them. At length, by mere accident, I discovered that he was in England, living obscurely in a mean village, married, Willis! and, as if to give point and poignancy to his disrespect, without even the form of asking the consent and approbation of me, his only relation, his friend, his benefactor—

Wil. How, sir!—did he not write letter after letter, complaining of your neglect of him? Did he not entreat, implore your sanction to his marriage?—till wearied at last by your continued silence, he became fully warranted in deciding for himself.

Wit. The goodness of your own nature suggests these excuses for his misconduct. He did, indeed, sometimes write to me, but in such terms, Willis—

Wil. Where are those letters, sir?

Wit. Mrs. Subtle, in kindness towards the reprobate, destroyed them the moment she read them to me.

Wil. She read them! Did you not, yourself, read them, sir?

Wit. No, the good soul spared me that pain; and, as Grasp has since told me, she even suppressed the most offensive passages.

Wil. Oh, infamy!

Wit. Aye, question me now, what grounds there are for my displeasure; but when I add that he has disgraced me by his worthless choice, that the woman he is married to is—

Wil. Hold, sir! I can hear no more! Your nephew may deserve your bitterest reproaches, but—

Wit. Hush! here comes Mrs. Subtle and Grasp. When you, a stranger to me, can with difficulty restrain your indignation, what must be mine?

Wil. (*Aside.*) My poor Marian! We must endure this yet awhile.

Enter MRS. SUBTLE *and* GRASP, L.

Mrs. S. Now, sir, it is your hour for walking. I have brought you your hat and cane.

Wit. Ever attentive, Mrs. Subtle; thankye, thankye. Well, Grasp, have you got that fifty pounds I asked you for?

Gra. Yes—but I can't think what you want them for; I have been plagued enough to procure money for our regular outlayings, and now—

Wit. That ought not to be; for surely I do not spend to the extent of my income; yet when I desire a small sum for any private purpose, you pretend—

Gra. Do you suppose that I take your money?

Wit. No, Grasp, no—but—

Gra. You are for ever drawing money for these idle uses. Five pounds for this poor family, ten for that—

Wit. Well, well, you are an old servant, and I believe faithfully attached to my interests; but I wish you would correct your manner.

Mrs. S. Indeed, Mr. Grasp, you should endeavour to moderate your tone; to use more respect when you address our good master (*takes Witherton's hand*)—our kind friend.

Wit. Ah, Mrs. Subtle! you are a worthy creature, and one of these days you may find that I am not ungrateful. (*To Grasp, mildly.*) Give that money to Willis; I shall direct him in the disposal of it.

Gra. I had better give up my accounts to him, my place. Till lately it has been my business to manage your money affairs. However, I have no notion of an interloper in the family, and either Mr. Willis or I must quit the house.

Wil. Do not let there be a source of discord here, sir.

Mrs. S. (*Artfully interposing between Grasp and Witherton, who is about to speak.*) Now—now—indeed, Mr. Grasp—you are wrong—(*to him*). You are going too far. (*To Witherton.*) Say nothing to him, sir—I will reprove him for this misconduct by-and-bye.

[*Grasp and Willis go up, C.*

Wit. But to treat me thus, and in the presence of Willis, too! Grasp, you will do as I desire. Willis, I must speak to you on my return. The day is fine, and a walk will do me good.

Mrs. S. Will you be very much displeased if I offer you my arm to lean upon, sir?

Wit. Thankye, Mrs. Subtle, thankye. Come.

[*Grasp goes up and gives money to Willis as they are going off.*

Enter PRY, L.

Pry. Ha! how d'ye do, this morning? I hope I don't intrude?

Wit. No, Mr. Pry, no. (*Aside.*) How provoking! But have you anything particular to say to me just now?

Pry. No—nothing particular; only, as I have just been to fetch my umbrella, which I left last Monday to be mended—Monday—no; it must have been—yes, I'm right, it was Monday; I remember it by a remarkable circumstance, Mrs. Jones sent a tray of pies to the baker's—on a Monday, mind you.

Wit. And what was there remarkable in that, Mr. Pry?

Pry. Pies on a Monday! She is not over rich, you know, and as I happened to know she had pies on Sunday! Pies two days following, for a person in her circumstances, did seem rather odd, you know.

Wit. Well, that's no business of mine and, if you have nothing—

Pry. No! only I thought that in my way back, I might as well drop in and say how d'ye do. I say, Mrs. Subtle—(*she down* R. *corner*)—you are a judge—I don't think this a dear job for one and nine-pence. (*Opens his umbrella.*)

Mrs. S. I must give him a broad hint, or we shall be pestered with the tedious fool for an hour. Mr. Pry, I beg pardon, but Mr. Witherton was just going to take his customary walk.

Pry. There is nothing so good for the health as walking.

(*Goes up, brings down a chair in the centre, and sits.*)

Mrs. S. There! now he is fixed for the day.

Pry. That is to say, walking in moderation. I am a great walker myself—I once brought on a fit of the gout by it; I did, although some people would have it to be nothing but the rheumatiz. I have had the rheumatiz, too, and know the difference—elbows and knees, at the same time. I was in this position for three weeks—I was, I assure you, looking exactly like a goose, ready trussed for roasting.

Wit. Well, good day—you'll excuse me.

Pry. Certainly! If you are going down the road I'll walk with you.

Mrs. S. (*Coming between them.*) But we are not, sir.

Pry. No matter; I'll walk with you the other way—I have nothing to do.

Mrs. S. But we have something to speak about.

Pry. (R.) Ah, ah! Mrs. Subtle, you're a sly one. Wheedling yourself into the old gentleman's good graces, eh?

Mrs. S. (L. C.) Sir!

Pry. Well, don't be angry—I only spoke, you know.

Wit. Come, Mrs. Subtle, come, for we shall now get rid of him. Some other time I shall be glad to see you, sir.

[*Exeunt Mrs. Subtle and Witherton,* L.

Pry. Thankye; I'll drop in again by-and-bye—a pleasant walk. Well, Mr. Willis, and how do you do?

Wit. (*Comes down,* R.) Now it's my turn.

Pry. I say, Marian, Mrs. Subtle's assistant, is a very pretty young woman. I saw you, last night, walking together by the river-side, though you didn't see me. I followed you for nearly half an hour.

Wit. Followed us?

Pry. I could not, for the life of me, make out what you were talking about—you put your heads so close together. Not difficult to guess, eh? I don't think it would be quite the match for you, though.

Wit. (*Aside.*) Then he does not suspect she is my wife.

Pry. After all, she is but a sort of deputy house-keeper, and I am told you belong to a respectable family. Tolerably respectable, eh?

Wit. Mr. Paul Pry, if you can make it appear that it concerns you a thousandth part of a straw to know, I'll write the history of my birth, parentage, and education for your particular information. Good morning to you, Mr. Pry.

[*Exit,* R.

Pry. Good morning to you, Mr. Willis—that's an uncommon polite young man. You are bringing him up to succeed you, I suppose—eh, Mr. Grasp? No bad thing neither—you must have a very comfortable place here?

Gra. (L. C.) Pretty well, as times go.

Pry. Though, from your master taking this small [s]house, economy is the order of the day, I take it, eh?

Gra. You had better ask my master.

Pry. No; he'd take it impertinent, perhaps. Bless you, it is no business of mine, only it appears odd—neither chick nor child, and, whenever he dies, he'll cut up for a pretty round sum, eh? A hundred thousand—eighty, eh? And you, you cunning dog, I dare say you have laid by a few thousands. Now, between ourselves, if it is not asking an impertinent question——

Gra. Not at all. (*Looks at his watch.*) Exactly ten minutes past twelve. So I wish you good morning.

[*Crosses and exit,* R.

Pry. That's one of the strangest—— (*Looking about.*) Well, I can't say it is very polite of them to leave me here alone. If I were the least of a bore, now, it would be pardonable; but—— (*Looks at his watch.*) Well, it's only ten minutes after twelve, I declare. How long the day seems. What shall I do till dinner time? Let me see—I'll just drop in at—— (*Looking off.*) Oho! Is it so? Aha, my young spark—trying the lock of Colonel Hardy's garden gate. That's very mysterious! Egad, I'll soon find out what you want there. (*Running off and returning.*) I had like to have gone without my umbrella.

SCENE III.—*Colonel Hardy's Garden—Garden wall, extending across the stage from* U. E. R. *to* U. E. L., *with door in* L. C.—*Practicable house,* T. E. R.—*garden chairs,* S. E. L.—*Ladder against wing,* S. E. R.

Enter PHEBE *from house,* R.

Phe. Oh, dear!—oh, dear! here's another fine day, and not a single cloud in the heavens to give me a hope of the rainy weather setting in. Here, in this stupid village, at fifty miles from London, have Miss Eliza and I been vegetating three eternal months; and as the sky continues so vexatiously bright, and the barometer obstinately pointing at "set fair," I see no chance of a speedy return to dear, delightful town. Heigho! this fine season will be the death of me.

Enter ELIZA, *with a book, from house,* R.

Eli. Heigho!

Phe. Heigho! ay, that is the burthen of our melancholy song.

Eli. What day is it, Phebe?

(*Sits on chair,* R., *Phebe,* L.

Phe. Who can tell, miss? Days are so much alike in this dull place, that it may be yesterday, or to-morrow, for anything there is to mark the difference.

Eli. And has the country no charms for you, Phebe? the spreading foliage, the natural music of the birds instead of London cries, the sublime spectacle of the rising sun?

Phe. Very fine, I daresay: but one must get up so early in the morning to see it.

Eli. Early in the morning! When else would you see the sun rise, Phebe?

Phe. Going home from a masquerade, or a ball, late at night, miss. All that may be very pleasant to a romantic young lady like you, just returned from boarding-school; but for my part, if, indeed, one had a little agreeable society here——

Eli. Well, and so we have! there's my pa, there's Mr. Paul Pry drops in sometimes——

Phe. Mr. Paul Pry! charming company, indeed! (*Mimics him.*) "If it isn't an impertinent question." The last time he was here, he asked me such things that really I——

Eli. Then Mr. Witherton comes to see us occasionally.

Phe. When his housekeeper allows him. An old twaddler! No, miss that is not the sort of society I mean.

Eli. What do you mean, Phebe?

Phe. A lover, miss.

Eli. Oh, fie! (*They rise.*) If my pa were to hear you talk so.

Phe. And were you never in love, then?

Eli. No, Phebe; and my pa would be very angry if I were to fall in love without his leave. (*Aside.*) I'm afraid to trust her.

Phe. (*Aside.*) What yea-nay piece of innocence it is. Well, miss, I have no pa to be angry with me, and if a pretty young fellow were to fall in my way——

Eli. Ha' done, Phebe; I must not hear you talk so. As to company, you know my cousin Frank is coming home from sea in about a week. We have not seen him since he was quite a boy, and he'll be company for us.

Phe. And how are we to amuse ourselves for a week?

Eli. We may read, work, or sing.

Phe. And when we are tired of that, to vary our amusement, we may sing, work, or read.

SONG.—"*The Lover's Mistake.*"

A fond youth serenaded his love,
Who sleeping,—"Love never should sleep!"—
Her father was peeping above,—
"Oh, fathers, you never should peep!"
To his daughter's balcony he brought
Her monkey, in muslins arrayed;
The youth was o'erjoyed, for he thought
'Twas the form of his beautiful maid.

He gazed on the figure in white,
Whose nods gave new life to his hopes,
His heart throbbed with love and delight,
As he threw up the ladder of ropes;
His charmer hopp'd down it, and then
The happy delusion was o'er!
Girls often meet monkey-like men,
But man ne'er wooed monkey before.

From the window, enjoying the joke,
Her father feared danger no more;
And she by the bustle awoke,
Soon made her escape at the door.
"Come, come to your Rosa," she said,
"Unless you prefer my baboon;
And, pray, let your next serenade
Take place at the full of the moon."

Ah, me! a country life is unfit for a single woman, and as my last mistress, Lady Courtly, used to say, there are but three circumstances that can render it tolerable to be a married one:

Eli. And what are they?

Phe. Hedges very high, ditches wide and deep, and a husband passionately fond of hunting. (*A flute heard behind wall, c.* "Tell her I love her.")

Eli. (*Lets her book drop.*) Oh, dear me!

Phe. What's that?

Eli. That, Phebe, I suspect, is nothing but a

flute. (*Aside.*) I am sure that is his signal. How imprudent of him to come down here.

Phe. Nothing but a flute. Now, as flutes don't usually play of themselves, I suspect it must be something more.

Eli. Well, Phebe, I—I'll confide my secret to you; but you won't betray me. It is my Harry.

Phe. Your what?

Eli. My Harry.

Phe. So then, Miss Innocence, you have a Harry of your own. Well done, upon my word. And who is your Harry?

Eli. Harry Stanley, a lieutenant in the navy.

Phe. And where could you have become acquainted with him? You have not been from under your father's eye since you were at boarding school; and——

Eli. There it was, Phebe; he used to come there to see his sister Harriet; and one day we fell in love with each other.

Phe. (*Laughing.*) "Oh, fie, Phebe, if my pa were to hear you talk so." And pray ain't you ashamed to fall in love without your pa's leave?

Eli. No, Phebe, for he's very young and very handsome. He's only eighteen.

Phe. Now, miss, let me give you a word of serious advice. I won't betray your secret, I promise you; but let me recommend you to mention it yourself to your father; and if the young gentleman should prove a suitable match for you—I dare say——

Eli. Don't you speak of that. I dare not for the world. First of all, you know my pa has some other marriage in view for me; and then he is so passionate and peremptory——

Phe. And as abrupt and absolute as if he were commanding his regiment.

Har. (*Within the house,* S. E. R.) Eliza, where are you?

Phe. Bless me, here he comes.

Eli. If my Harry should repeat the signal, we shall be discovered.

Enter HARDY *from house,* R., *and comes down,* C.

Har. Eliza, my dear, I expect company to-day.

Eli. Do you, pa?

Har. My neighbour, Witherton, and a young gentleman I expect from London, to-day. He is the husband I intend for you. You'll be married in a week.

Eli. So soon, pa?

Har. Ay, and sooner, if by chance my nephew Frank should return. I daresay Frank has grown a giant. I long to see the boy; I have not seen him since he was nine years old.

Phe. (*L.*) But I believe, sir, my young lady has never seen the young gentleman you intend for her husband.

Har. What of that? she's no worse off than I am. I have not seen him. His father writes me word that he has a son, who is a prodigy, I reply, that my daughter is a miracle; the marriage is decided on, and who dares say anything against it? Do you, or do you? Nobody has anything to say against it. So much the better; all parties must be perfectly satisfied. (*Takes Eliza's hand.*) That's a good obedient girl.

Phe. (*Aside.*) Oh! the silly thing! I have not patience with her. Beg pardon, sir, but suppose—I merely say, suppose—Miss Eliza should happen not to love your intended son-in-law?

Har. What then? what is love? what has love to do with it? Did I marry her mother for love?

yet we were very happy together; at least, I can speak for myself. I was happy when I married her—happy while she lived—happy when she died; and I've been happy ever since, and that's worth all the love in the universe.

Phe. Some folks may not be of your way of thinking, sir.

Har. Think, indeed, you saucy baggage! what do you mean by thinking? Who gave you liberty to think? I allow nobody in my house to think. I am not like old Witherton, I expect obedience; so obey all of you, d'ye hear?

Eli. But, pa, if I might inquire the gentleman's name——

Phe. (*Aside.*) There's an effort.

Har. Hey-day! a mutiny in the regiment. If you had not asked, perhaps I'd have told you; now you shall know nothing about it; you shall not know who he is till you are under the hands of the parson. If you provoke me further you shall marry him blindfolded. May be, never know who he is. But I perceive what this is. (*To Phebe.*) It is you who have been putting these high romantic notions about loving a husband into my girl's head.

Phe. Desiring to know who her husband is to be is mighty romantic, truly. If, indeed, now she was to entertain a secret passion for some ardent youth who should serenade her by moonlight.

Har. She! she presume to fall in love without my consent! Look at her, bless her innocent heart! I tell you what, Miss Phebe, if I hear any more—but what was that you said about serenading? That reminds me—who was that playing the flute under my garden wall just now?

Phe. How should we know, sir? most likely some bird-catcher decoying the thrushes.

Har. Thrushes, indeed! No, no, it was not the thrushes he was decoying. Some flirtation of yours, I daresay, and I won't allow it.

Phe. Mine, indeed, sir! I am no more capable of such a thing than my young lady herself.

Har. Say no more on the subject. It is setting a bad example to my daughter, and I won't allow it, I tell you. Come with me, my dear; and hark'ye, Miss Phebe, your bird-catcher had better take care I don't catch him. (*As he is going, a stone with a letter attached to it is thrown over the wall.*) What's that?

Eli. Oh, Phebe! what will become of me?

Har. What's that, I say?

Phe. That, sir—why can't you see what it is? A stone some idle boy has thrown over the wall.

Har. I say, you idle boy, how dare you throw stones? Why! there's a letter tied to it! Stand out of the way and let me have it. No address!

Phe. (*Aside.*) That's fortunate. Give it to me, sir, it is mine.

Har. Yours, is it? we shall soon see that. (*Crosses to c.*) Why, what a scrawl—and in pencil, too (*reads.*) "Loveliest of your sex."

Phe. (*L.*) There, sir, I told you it was addressed to me.

Har. You, indeed, you ugly little monkey—are you the loveliest of your sex?

Phe. 'Tis quite clear it is not for you, sir; so give it to me.

Har. Will somebody stop that girl's tongue? Let me read (*reads*). "Persuaded you would recognise the signal, and attend to it, I had determined to scale the garden wall, but am prevented by an impertinent fellow who is watching my

movements. An interview is indispensable, as I have something of the deepest importance to communicate. When he is gone, I will return. Has your father "—your father!—"any suspicion of our mutual attachment? Your eternally devoted."—No signature, so the case is evident. (*To Eliza, R.*) Now, Miss Timidity; you, with your demure looks—you, who have never had an answer beyond "Yes, pa," and "No, pa," and can scarcely say "Bo to a goose"—what can you find to say to this?—Answer me—who is this bird-catcher of yours? Speak, I say!

Eli. Indeed, pa, I—!

Phe. Don't answer, miss: if you have any secret of your own, you may do as you please about it; but you have no right to divulge mine.

Har. Yours! don't attempt to deceive me—her looks convict her—besides, am not I her father mentioned here?

Phe. No, sir—it is my father.

Har. Your father! How the devil came you by a father? Who ever heard of your father?

Phe. I imagine I have as good a right to a father as my betters!—at any rate that letter is mine. The appointment was with me; and if you was twenty times my master, I would protest against your competency to intercept my correspondence.

Har. Why, zounds! here's a chambermaid talking like a member of parliament—but I'll presently come to the truth of this, and if I find you to blame, (*to Eliza*) I'll lock you up on bread and water till you're married; and your husband shall do the same by you for the rest of your life afterwards. But how to proceed?—I have it. The fellow, whoever he is, intends to return; no doubt he is still lurking about. Stay you where you are, don't move, and if either of you utter a sound, or give the slightest signal, woe be to you.

(*Places ladder against wall, mounts, and looks cautiously over.*)

Eli. Phebe, Phebe, my poor Harry will be discovered, and what are we to do then?

Phe. What indeed, miss! but it is your own fault. If you had admitted me to your confidence, I could have managed matters much better I promise you.

Har. (*Descending.*) I have him—there he is, crouching on the ground with his eye at the keyhole: he shall find me a more expert bird-catcher than himself, for I'll catch him first—and hang me, but I'll salt his tail for him afterwards. (*Hardy suddenly opens the garden gate, and discovers Pry in the attitude described; he seizes him by the collar, and drags him down, c.*) I have you, you villain! Come in, and let me hear what you have to say for yourself. Who are you? What do you want here?

Eli. (*R. to Phebe.*) Why, 'tis Mr. Pry.

Phe. (*R. C.*) Then we are safe.

Har. Speak, I say—who are you?

Pry. You know I can't speak if you choke me.

Har. I have something worse than choking for you—who are you?

Pry. Why, don't you know me? Mr. Pry—Paul Pry!

Har. And so it is. So then, you are the bird-catcher, you rascal!

Pry. Bless you, no, I'm no bird-catcher—I'm——

Har. And it is thus you abuse my hospitality? Is it for this, you are constantly dropping in? Confess the truth, or you shall drop in where you little expect before you are five minutes older.

Pry. What is it you mean?

Har. Is it the mistress or the maid?

Pry. Are you out of your senses?

Har. You think I'm in the dark; but I'll convince you I have detected your intrigue. (*Shows the stone.*) What's this?

Pry. That!

Har. No equivocation—what is it?

Pry. Why, I should take it to be a stone.

Har. Oh—you confess that—and what's this? (*Shows the note.*)

Pry. It looks like a note.

Har. A note! very well. But I have not done with you yet—you have others about you. (*Chasing him round to* L.) What have you done with your flute?

Pry. (*Presenting his umbrella.*) What you have done with your senses?

Phe. I wonder your are not ashamed of yourself, Mr. Pry, to send letters to me, and compromise a young woman's reputation as you have done.

Pry. I—upon my life, I never compromised a young woman since the day I was born.

Phe. (*Making signs to him.*) If you mean honourable towards me, speak to my father, otherwise your playing the flute is playing the fool, that I can tell you.

Pry. Oh, I perceive you mistake me for the young man I surprised here just now.

Har. What, what—a young man—then it wasn't you?

Pry. Lord, no. I'll tell you all about it! (*Familiarly taking Hardy's arm, who indignantly throws him off.*)

Har. Do, then, and be quick.

Phe. Devil take the chattering booby.

Pry. You must know that I was coming from Mr. Witherton's, where I had just dropt in to ask him how his tooth was—now that's very provoking, I forgot to ask him after all.

Har. Never mind the tooth now.

Pry. It's a double tooth.

Har. Out with it.

Pry. Yes, I advised him to have it out.

Har. Get on with your story.

Pry. And just as I was turning the corner, I perceived a young man preparing to climb your wall. The instant he saw me, away he ran—Oho! thinks I——

Har. Oh, the tiresome——In a word, then, he has escaped.

Pry. He ran away, as I said—and that is all I know of the matter.

Har. And what were you doing there?

Pry. Eh! why, to tell you the truth, I heard a talking here; and as I could not make out what the meaning of it all was, and one is naturally anxious to know, you know! I just took the liberty to put my ear to the key-hole, then I put my eye. (*Puts his hand to his eye.*) There again? I shan't be able to see out of this eye for a week. I hate these plaguey small keyholes, the wind comes through them like a needle.

Har. So, then, you confess you have been caves-dropping about my house. Not content with coming inside perpetually to see what is going forward, you must go prying and peeping about outside. Harkee, Mr. Pry, you are a busy, meddling, curious, impertinent——

Pry. It is not genteel to call names. Indeed I think you ought to be obliged to me for the discovery.

Har. And what have you discovered? But it is your way. You never get hold of a story, but you take it at the wrong end. But for your busy interference the fellow would have carried his intention into execution, and I should have had him.

Pry. Well, I did it for the best; but if ever I do a good-natured thing again! (*Picks up book and returns to garden seat,* S. E. L.)

Har. 'Tis clear there is something going forward. (*To Eliza.*) But now that my suspicions are excited, I'll watch you closely, and if I find you concerned in it—— (*Leading Eliza up to house,* R.)

Eli. Indeed, pa——

Har. Well, well, I'm not to be deceived, so beware. [*Exit Eliza into house.* As to you, you imp of mischief, I'll answer for it, you are in the plot, whatever it is.

Phe. That is the rule in these cases, the mistress can do no wrong; so we poor ministers of waiting-women are made the scape-goats.

Har. (*To Phebe.*) You get in. [*Exit Phebe,* S. E. R. (*To Pry who is seated on the garden chair, reading.*) And you get out. (*Opens the door.*)

Pry. This is a mysterious affair—most mysterious. I shan't sleep a wink till I have discovered what it is all about.

Har. Are you coming, sir?

Pry. Beg pardon, Colonel—I wish you a very good morning! [*Exit,* D.

Har. Good morning, good morning. The meddling blockhead! Can this have been an assignation with my daughter? No, no, she is too innocent, too artless—'tis some love affair of Phebe's, no doubt. However, I'll have an eye on both of them. (*A loud ring at bell.*) Who's that I wonder. (*Opens door, and Pry appears at gate.*)

Pry. (*Going to the garden chair.*) Beg pardon! forgot my umbrella, that's all.

Har. Plague take you and your umbrella! [*Hardy seizes the garden rake, and aims a blow at Pry, who exits hastily at gate.*

END OF ACT I.

ACT II.

SCENE I.—*Room at Witherton's. Verandah window opening to garden,* L. *in* F.; *door in* F. R.

Enter WILLIS *and* MARIAN, R.

Wil. Yet a little forbearance, dear Marian, and all will be well.

Mar. Would our fate were decided, for even in my assumed character I find it difficult to endure the tyranny and insolence of Mrs. Subtle. The struggle is severe between the affected submission of the supposed dependent and the real indignation of the wife of Edward Somers.

Wil. I, too, have a difficult part to play. This morning I nearly betrayed myself to my uncle. His reproaches of me, undeserved as they were, I listened to unmoved—but when he would have censured you—fortunately at that moment we were interrupted, so our secret is still secure.

Mar. Upon the whole, Edward, I cannot but

consider this scheme of our friend, Colonel Hardy, as rather a wild one.

Wil. Yet hitherto it has succeeded. Here as a stranger, and in the character of an humble companion, I have won from my uncle that affection which the intrigues of an artful woman have diverted from me as his nephew; you are also no little favourite with him. Thus the main point is gained by the destruction of a prejudice unfavourable to us.

Mar. What more have you discovered of Grasp and Mrs. Subtle?

Wil. Sufficient to confirm our suspicions that letters, from and to me, have been intercepted by them. I have reason, too, to believe that Mrs. Subtle's grand project is a marriage with my uncle —by the influence she would thus obtain over him our ruin would be accomplished.

Mar. And are there no means of preventing their marriage?

Wil. I fear it will be difficult! when the affections of a solitary old man, a slave like him to circumstance and habit, are once entangled in the snares of a wily woman, it is no easy task to disengage them. But here she and my uncle come— we must not be seen together. Ha! 'tis too late —they are here.

Enter WITHERTON, *leaning on* MRS. SUBTLE'S *arm*, L.

Mrs. S. Gently, sir, gently. (*To Marian.*) What are you doing here? Why are you not in your own apartment?

Mar. I—I was merely talking to Mr. Willis, ma'am.

Mrs. S. Leave the room.

Wil. Speak mildly to her, my good Mrs. Subtle; consider—she is young and timid.

Mrs. S. Young and timid, indeed!

Wil. Go, my dear; Mrs. Subtle is a little severe in manner, but she means well.

Mar. (*Crosses to* L.) I obey you, sir.

Mrs. S. (*In an undertone.*) Obey *me*, or count not on a long continuance here—begone!

[*Exit Marian,* L.

Leave her to me, sir, I understand these matters best. (*To Willis, in a gentler tone.*) And you, Mr. Willis, to encourage a forward chit like that—I'm astonished at you.

Wil. Indeed, you mistake me.

Mrs. S. No matter, leave us.

Wit. Be within call, Willis, I would speak with you presently.

Wil. I will, sir.

[*Exit,* S. E. R.

(*Mrs. Subtle brings a chair foward for Witherton, who seats himself* L. *of Mrs. Subtle.*)

Wit. That girl is a favourite of mine, Mrs. Subtle, in her way—in her way, I mean. She was strongly recommended to me by my friend, Colonel Hardy, and I am sorry you have conceived so strange an antipathy against her.

Mrs. S. And I am surprised you are so strongly attached to her. Do you know I am almost—I had nearly said a foolish word—jealous of her?

Wil. Jealous! Now, Mrs. Subtle, you would banter me. But now we are alone, and secure from interruption, tell me what it is you would consult me upon—once while we were out you were on the point of speaking, when we were in-

truded upon by that meddling blockhead, Mr. Pry.

Mrs. S. Oh, 'tis nothing, sir—a trifle.

Wil. You cannot deceive me; something sits heavily at your heart; explain the cause of it—you know me for your friend, your sincere friend. Come, speak freely.

Mrs. S. Well, then, sir; since I never act in any important matter but by your direction, I would ask your advice in this, of all others, the—most important.

Wit. Go on.

Mrs. S. Mr. Grasp, who has long been attentive to me, has at length become importunate for my decision on the question of marriage.

Wit. Marriage! Take a chair, Mrs. Subtle; take a chair.

Mrs. S (*Sits.*) Yes, sir. Hitherto I have never distinctly accepted, nor have I rejected the offer of his hand; wearied at length by my indecision, he has this morning insisted on knowing my intentions, one way or the other.

Wit. Well, well.

Mrs. S. It is a serious question; my mind is still unsettled; my heart, alas! takes no part in the question. How would you advise me, sir?

Wit. Really, Mrs. Subtle, I was so little prepared for such a communication, that I hardly know— Grasp is an honest man—a very honest man.

Mrs. S. He is a very honest man, yet my own experience has taught me that a very honest man may be a very—very bad husband. Then, although I allow Mr. Grasp to be a very well-meaning man —his temper—

Wit. That is none of the best, certainly.

Mrs. S. His manners, too—not that I believe he would willingly offend—are offensive. Even you, I fear, have observed that, for he has frequently addressed you in a mode which my affection—I would say, my respect for you has induced me to reprove.

Wit. He does lack urbanity, I grant.

Mrs. S. And to me that is intolerable, for, notwithstanding my situation here, I can never forget that I am the daughter of a gentleman. Then his tastes and habits differ from mine.

Wit. These are important objections, Mrs. Subtle, considering that your first husband was as you have told me.

Mrs. S. Speak not to me of him, sir, for that reminds me of one of the bitterest periods of my life. Yet, spite of Mr. Subtle's ill-usage of me, I never once forgot the duty and obedience of a wife; but he was young, vain, fickle, and I am too late convinced that it is not till a man is somewhat advanced in life—till his sentiments and habits are formed and fixed, that he can thoroughly appreciate the value of a wife's affections, or so regulate his conduct as to insure her happiness and his own.

Wit. That is a very sensible remark, Mrs. Subtle.

Mrs. S. My father was an evidence of the truth of it, sir. My father was nearly sixty when he married.

Wit. Indeed! your own father?

Mrs. S. Ay, sir, and he lived to the good old age of eighty-seven. But he was happy, and enjoyed a contented mind. How tenderly my poor mother loved him!

Wit. What was her age?

Mrs. S. When she married him, about mine, sir.

I believe it was the contemplation of the picture of their felicity, so constantly before my eyes, that confirmed my natural disposition for the quiet of domestic life. Ah, had I been fortunate in the selection of a partner!

Wit. Much—everything depends on that, and I think that Grasp is not altogether—he is not at all, the husband for you.

Mrs. S. So my heart tells me, sir; yet, when I quit your house, would you have me live alone, without a protector?

Wit. How—quit my house.

Mrs. S. Alas! that I must, whether I accept this proposal or not. Yet let not that distress you, sir, for I doubt not—I hope, that when I am gone, my place may be supplied by someone equally attentive to your comforts—your happiness.

Wit. Do I hear aright? Quit my house, and wherefore?

Mrs. S. I hardly know in what words to tell you; and, after all, perhaps you will say I am a silly woman to regard such idle slander. Who can control the tongue of scandal? My care of you, my attentions, my unceasing assiduities, become the subject of remark (I had resolved not to mention this to you), but my unwearied attention to you, which is the result of mere duty—of friendship—perhaps of a sisterly affection, is said to spring from a deeper—a warmer source——

Wit. And were it so, dear Mrs. Subtle, are we accountable to a meddling world——

Mrs. S. Ah, sir, you, a man strong in the rectitude of your conduct, master of your own actions, I say, and independent of the world, may set aside its busy slanders. But I, a humble, unprotected woman!—no, the path of duty lies straight before me; I must give my hand where I feel I cannot bestow my heart, and for ever quit a house where I have been but too happy.   (*Appears affected.*)

Wit. Nay, by heaven, but you shall not; must your happiness be sacrificed? Mine, too?—Ay, mine.

Mrs. S. (*Rises.*) Hold, sir, say no more. Do not prolong a delusion which I am endeavouring to dispel. If I have unwarily betrayed to you a secret—which I have scarcely dared to trust even to my own thoughts; if I have foolishly mistaken the kindness of a friend for a more tender sentiment, pardon my presumption, and forgive her, who, but for the lowliness of her station, might as an affectionate and devoted wife, have administered to your happiness; and who, conscious of her own unworthiness, must soon behold you for the last time.   (*Going, in tears.*)

Wit. Stay, dearest Mrs. Subtle, and listen to your friend, your best and truest friend. First promise me that here you will remain.

Mrs. S. But you have not yet advised me respecting Mr. Grasp's proposal, and I have promised him an immediate reply.

Wit. Attend to what I am about to say, and then dearest Mrs. Subtle, let you own heart dictate your choice.

Mrs S. (*Aside.*) 'Tis done!

Wit. Were I no longer to hesitate, I should be negligent of my own happiness, and unjust towards your merits; for if an attachment, long and severely tried, were not of itself sufficient to warrant me in——   (*A knock at the door, R.*)

Mrs. S. (*As Witherton starts up.*) Curse on the interruption, when but another word had realised my hopes.

Enter PAUL PRY, L.

Pry. Oh, ah, I see, billing and cooing—I hope I don't intrude?

Mrs. S. You do, sir.

Pry. Well, I'm very sorry, but I came to show you the "County Chronicle;" there's something in it I thought might interest you; two columns, full, about a prodigious gooseberry, grown by Mrs. Nettlebed, at the Priory. Most curious; shall I read it to you?

Wit. No, you are very good.
    (*Turns up impatiently.*)

Pry. I perceive I am one too many. Well, now, upon my life, (*whispers her*) if I had entertained the smallest idea——

Mrs. S. What do mean, sir?

Pry. Bless you, I see things with half an eye; but never fear me, I'm as close as wax. Now, I say Mrs. Subtle, between ourselves—it shall go no farther, there is something in the wind, eh?

Mrs. S. I don't understand you.

Pry. Well, well, you are right to be cautious; only I have often thought to myself it would be a good thing for both of you, he is rich—no one to inherit his fortune, and by all accounts, you have been very kind to him, eh?

Mrs. S. Sir!

Pry. I mean no harm, but take my advice; service is no inheritance, as they say. Have you looked to number one? Taken care to feather your nest? You are still a young woman?—under forty, I should think?—thirty-eight now?—there, or thereabouts, eh?

Mrs. S. My respect for Mr. Witherton forbids me to say that his friend is impertinent.

Wit. This intrusion is no longer to be borne. (*Comes down L. of Pry.*) Have you any particular business with me sir?

Pry. Yes, you must know, I've seen a young fellow lurking about your friend Hardy's house, and I suspect there is something not right going forward in his family.

Wit. That is his business, not mine, sir.

Pry. True, but I have been thinking that as you are his friend, it would be but friendly if you were just to drop in, and talk to him about it.

Wit. That is my business, and not yours.

Pry. I don't say the contrary, but at all events, I'm determined to keep watch over——

Wit. That is your business, therefore you may do as you please; yet let me suggest to you, that this unhappy propensity of yours, to meddle in matters which do not concern you, may one day or other produce very mischievous effects.

Pry. Now I take that as unkind; what interest have I in trying to do a good-natured thing? am I ever a gainer by it? But I'll make a vow, that from this time forward I will never interfere. Hush, there he is again; will you do me a favour? just allow me to go out this way.

Wit. Any way out you please.

Pry. I'll give the alarm, and if I let him escape me this time—Follow! follow! follow!
    [*Exit D. in R. F.*

HARRY STANLEY *appears at the window, L.*

Har. Confound him! the same officious booby again.

Pry. (*Without.*) Now, my lively spark, I'll have you.

Har. Egad, you shall run for it, then.
    [*Runs off, Pry after him.*

Wit. What can be the meaning of all this! That busy fellow's interruption has thrown all my ideas into confusion.

Mrs. S. Be composed, sir; take a chair, and let us resume——

Enter GRASP, abruptly, R.

Well, what is it you want, Mr. Grasp?

Gra. You!

Wi. Mrs. Subtle is engaged just now.

Gra. No matter, she must come with me, I have something to say to her.

Mrs. S. I'll come to you presently.

Gra. You must come at once. I am not to be made a dupe—come. Mr. Willis is waiting to see you in the library, sir—now, Mrs. Subtle, if you please.

[Crosses and Exit, L.

Wit. Return quickly, dear Mrs. Subtle, and promise nothing till you have again consulted me.

Mrs S. I will obey you, sir; you see how easily we poor weak women are diverted from our better resolutions.

[Exit Witherton, R.

He is mine. What can have angered Grasp? near as are my schemes to their completion, one word from that man might yet destroy them all. Has he overheard us? Does he suspect what is my project? I must contrive still to evade him, till I have made Witherton securely mine. Then let him do his worst.

[Exit, L.

SCENE II.—*A Room at Hardy's. Door, S. E. R.; an open window, T. E. L.*

Cries without of "Follow! follow!"—Enter ELIZA and PHEBE, R.

Eli. Oh, Phebe! Phebe! what can be the cause of all this confusion?

Phe. Confusion, indeed, miss, one would think the very de—Old Harry had broken loose.

Eli. Old Harry, Phebe—I'm very much afraid it's young Harry.

Phe. You see now the consequences of your imprudence, miss.

Eli. If it should really be my poor Harry, and my pa should discover him.

Phe. Mercy on us all; and now his suspicions are awakened, and his anger excited by this morning's adventure, he will be less tractable than ever. (*Cries of "Follow! follow!"*)

Enter HARRY STANLEY at the window, T. E. L.

Har. (R.) Any port in a storm, so here I am. What, my sweet little Eliza here! this is beyond my hopes.

Eli. Oh, Mr. Stanley, how could you be so imprudent?

Har. Now, my dear, sweet, pretty little Eliza, don't be angry with me—allow me a minute to recover breath, and I'll tell you about it. This run has been a breather.

Phe. What a pretty little fellow he is; I should have no objection to just such another little lover for myself.

Eli. But, tell me quickly, how came you here?

Har. By no very smooth path, I promise you; by scaling a twelve-feet wall, leaping across a canal, climbing an apple-tree, and so in at the first-floor window.

Eli. But why venture to come into the house?

Har. Why, once over the garden wall, egad, I had no time to choose; my manoeuvre was detected by that same prying scoundrel who prevented our interview this morning—let him fall in my way, and I'll snip his ears for him. He gave the alarm, and in an instant every servant in the place, to the very dairymaid, was in full chase of me. I flew like a skiff before the wind, and cleared the canal at a leap. None of my pursuers could weather that point, so finding myself a few minutes ahead of them, and perceiving that window open, I made all sail for it as my only chance of escape, and here I am.

Phe. (L.) You have escaped with a vengeance. Do you know, sir, where you are?

Har. (R.) In the presence of my darling little Eliza, and where else could I be so happy?

Eli. (C.) Did you hear that, Phebe?

Phe. Pooh! nonsense, we are all on the very brink of ruin, and there he is quietly talking about being happy. You must instantly quit this place, so get out how you can. (*Goes up to the window.*)

Har. No, no; I have had so much trouble to get in, that I'll not get out again till I have explained my errand.

Eli. What Phebe says is true; if my pa should come——

Phe. (*Comes forward to L.*) They are on a wrong scent, so you are safe for a few minutes; but speak quickly.

Har. First tell me, when do you expect your cousin Frank?

Eli. Not for a week.

Har. That will be too late, as Frank, who is my old shipmate and friend, would have interceded for us with your father.

Phe. But since he is not here, what next do you propose?

Har. Boldly to ask the Colonel's consent.

Phe. Which he will refuse.

Har. So I expect, and am prepared accordingly. Now, I have a most important question to ask you —pray, ladies, are you fond of travelling?

Eli. What an odd question!

Har. I have just seen in Doubledot's yard the prettiest yellow postchaise in the world. (*Puts his arms round their waists.*) It will just hold us three as comfortably as if it had been made for us. We clap four horses to it, visit the blacksmith, get married, and then let our pa's unmarry us if they can.

Eli. Why, Harry, that would be running away, and I must not think of such a thing.

Phe. Oh, that somebody would make me such an offer.

Har. Running away! look at me, I've just been running away, and I am nothing the worse for it.

Eli. You!

Har. I had scarcely arrived at my father's house when the old gentleman told me of some dowdy of his own choosing, whom he intended I should marry. I ventured a respectful remonstrance; he swore I should marry her; if I do, sir, says I, I'll be—(*Phebe stops his mouth.*) So I cut short the argument by mounting a horse and galloping down here.

Phe. Then I'd advise you to remount him and gallop home again, for my young lady is in a precisely similar situation. The Colonel has provided a husband for her, and——

Har. In that case an elopement is our only resource; and if our dear pa's are determined on a marriage, we'll leave them to marry one another.

Phe. That's all very fine, but you must go—so take the first opportunity whilst the coast is clear. You are a very imprudent young gentleman, and I foresee mischief unless I take the management of this affair into my own hands. If you would have me for a friend, begone at once, and I'll do all I can to serve you.

Har. You are a good little girl, and if I don't contrive to find you a husband too. (*To Eliza.*) One kiss, and I'm gone. I must not forget my little Bridget—Abigail—what's her name?
                              (*Kisses Phebe.*)

Phe. Phebe! Phebe!—there, sir, that will do.

Eli. (*Dragging him away.*) There, Phebe says that will do : so you had better go, Harry.
        (*As he is going, Hardy speaks without,* L.)

Har. Don't leave a bush or a bramble unsearched, let loose Jupiter and Bacchus! and whoever the villain is, bring him before me dead or alive.

Phe. There's a pretty business! The Colonel is coming—quick—jump out of the window, 'tis the way you came in.

Har. But coming and going are two very different things, Mrs. Phebe; no, I'll remain here, and declare my intentions.

Eli. Oh, no—I wouldn't have my pa see you for the world.

Phe. Here—quick—this way.
        (*She pushes him into room,* S. E. R., *and stands before the door.*).

Eli. What have you done? consider, that is my room.

Phe. No matter, miss—we'll conceal him there till your father is gone, and then I'll contrive to get him away.

Enter HARDY, *with brace of pistols,* L. C. *doors.*

Har. (*Speaking off.*) Stand you at the staircase, and the first person that attempts to pass without my orders, fire; this time he shall not escape me. So, here you are—what have you to say for yourselves? Which of you is the culprit?

Phe. What do you mean, sir?

Har. But I perceive—there she stands, pale and trembling. Come hither, and tell me who he is.

Eli. Indeed, pa, you frighten me so, I cannot speak.

Har. Frightened. How dare you be frightened when your tender, kind old father speaks to you? Zounds, am I Blackcard or the Grand Turk? but tell me who he is, I say.

Phe. Who, sir?

Har. A man has been seen to come over my garden wall.

Phe. Ha! ha! ha! and is that all? So for that the whole house is in an uproar; as if the orchard had never been robbed before.

Har. What, at noonday!

Phe. Why then, sir, it is some visitor of your own, perhaps.

Har. Would any visitor of mine come scrambling over the wall when I have a door to my house? But they'll catch him, and then——come hither, Phebe, and tell me the truth; if my daughter has deceived me, do you tell me, and spare me the mortification of exposing her misconduct in the presence of every menial in my service.

Eli. (R., *Aside.*) Don't betray me, Phebe.

Phe. (R. C.) You are so passionate, sir, that even if I knew——

Cries of "Follow! follow!" *and barking of dogs at* L. U. E.

Pry. (*Without window,* T. E L.) Would you murder me, you hard-hearted monster?

Har. (*Going up stage.*) They have him—they have him.

Pry. (*With one foot at the window and speaking off.*) Don't fire! I'm a friend of the family, I tell you! oh, if I do but escape with my life!
        (*Hardy points pistol at Pry.*)

Phe. (*Aside.*) Then we are saved again.
                              (*Pry tumbles in.*)

Har. (*Giving him his hand.*) Pray do me the honour to walk in, sir. So this is the second time I have you. Now what rigmarole story can you invent?   (*Shaking him.*)

Pry. Let me go—there's a mistake—I'm not the man—I'm your friend. I was coming this way, intending just to drop in, when——

Har. (L. C.) My friend, indeed! (*Places pistol on table,* T. E. L.) How dare any friend of mine drop in at the first-floor window?

Pry. (L.) If you doubt my friendship, see what I have suffered in your service.
        (*Turns about and shows his clothes torn.*)

Har. Explain yourself.

Pry. I have been hunted like a stag, and nearly sacrificed like a heathen to the fury of Jupiter and Bacchus—and all owing to a mistake. I saw a strange man climb over your wall; and being naturally anxious to know what he could want, I followed him—gave the alarm—and——

Phe. (R. C.) Why, this is the same story he told us this morning, sir.

Har. And so it is. Why, this is the same story you told me this morning!—harkee, sir; if you find no better excuse for your extraordinary conduct, I shall forget you are my neighbour, act in my quality of magistrate, and commit you for the trespass. I find you entering my house in a very suspicious manner——

Pry. Well, if ever I do a good-natured turn again. Let me tell you, Colonel, that you are treating me like a phœnix—a thing I am not used to.

Har. What do you mean by treating you like a phœnix?

Pry. Tossing me out of the frying-pan into the fire. What I tell you is true. I gave the alarm, but the fellow was so nimble that he escaped; while your servants, seeing me run as if I had been running for a wager, mistook me for the man—set the dogs after me—and in short—I am well off to have escaped with my life.

Har. If this be true, what has become of the other?—The gates are closed, and——

Pry. He's safe enough, I'll answer for it—though I could not overtake him, I never lost sight of him. (*Observing a signal made by Phebe.*) Oho! that explains the mystery—some swain of Miss Phebe's.

Har. What has become of him, I say? I'll not be trifled with—you are the only trespasser I discover, and will commit *you* unless——

Pry. Oh, if that's the case (you need not nod and wink at me, ladies), the matter is growing serious, and I have already suffered sufficiently. He's here, Colonel, I saw him get in at that window!

Phe. Oh, the wretch! a likely story—a man get in at that window, and we not see him?

Pry. Well, who says you didn't see him?

Phe. Why, we have not been out of the room this half-hour—have we, miss?

Har. Do you hear that?—a likely story, indeed! If you saw him, describe him?

Pry. Describe him! How can I describe him? I tell you he was running like a greyhound—he didn't wait for me to take his portrait! He got up at that window, and I'll swear he didn't get down again; so here he must be. (*Walks up and round the stage, and looks under the sofa and table.*)

Phe. It is a pity, Mr. Pry, you have no business of your own to employ you. Ah, that's right, look about here. You had better search for him in my young lady's reticule. (*Snatches reticule from Eliza.*)

Pry. Stand aside, Mrs. Phebe, and let me—— (*Opening* D. R.)

Phe. Why, you abominable person—that is Miss Eliza's room; how dare you open the door? (*Throwing him round by collar to* c.)

Har. You abominable person! how dare you open my daughter's room door?—(*Throwing him round by collar to* L.)

Pry. If there's no one concealed there, why object?

Har. True. If there's no one concealed there, why object?

Phe. I wonder, sir, you allow of such an insinuation. (*Places herself at the door,* s. E. R.) No one shall enter this room; we stand here upon our honour; and if you suspect my young lady's, what is to become of mine, I should like to know?

Pry. Can't possibly say; but I would advise you to look after it, for I protest he is there.

Har. (*Endeavouring to suppress his anger.*) Sir, you are impertinent. It cannot be, and I desire you will quit my house. Simon!

Enter SIMON, L.

Simon, open the door for Mr. Pry.

Phe. Simon, you are to open the door for Mr. Pry.

Pry. Oh! I dare say Simon hears, I wish you a very good morning—I expect to be asked to dinner for this at least—this is most mysterious. I say, Simon?

[*Exit, whispering, Simon,* L.

Har. (*Who has taken a brace of pistols from a case on the table.*) I would not expose you in the presence of that busy fool; but now, whoever he is, he shall answer his outrage to me.

Eli. (R.) Oh, pa, for heaven's sake. I'll tell you the truth.

Phe. (L.) Yes, sir, we will tell you. (*Aside.*) What shall I say?

Har. (c.) Tell me at once, hussey—is there a man in the room?

Phe. Why, then, sir, there is a sort of a young man, to be sure—but——

Har. But what?

Phe. But don't be angry, for he is the prettiest little fellow you ever saw.

Har. A little fellow? A man is concealed in my house, and because he happens not to be the Irish giant, I must not be angry. Oh! that my nephew, Frank, were at home: but I'm still young enough to——

Phe. Stay, sir. (*Aside.*) Anything to gain time and prevent murder. You have guessed it, it is your nephew, Mr. Frank.

Har. What, Frank? my boy, Frank?

Phe. Yes, sir, arrived a week earlier than was expected. We, Miss Eliza and I, sir—we were in the secret, and had planned a little surprise for you, but that eternal Mr. Pry spoiled it.

Har. (*Places pistols on the table.*) Oh, you wicked little rebels, to cause me so much uneasiness—but let me see the dear boy—let me——

Phe. Stop, sir, I'll just inform him that——

Har. Don't detain me an instant. (*Going towards the door.*) What, Frank, come to your old uncle, you dog—why, zounds! what is he at now? scarcely is he in at one window but he is preparing to jump out at another.

[*Exit,* s. E. R.

Eli. Phebe, what have you done? my pa must soon detect the imposture, and then——

Phe. Lord, miss, what would have been the consequence if the Colonel, in that storming passion, and with pistols in his hands, had been told the truth. We may yet get your Harry safe out of the house, and then—hush!

Enter HARDY, *pulling in* HARRY STANLEY, s. R. R.

Har. Come, Frank, an end to this foolery. Phebe has explained it all to me: I'm devilish glad to see you, and that is worth all the surprise in the world.

Harry. Sir—I—what is the meaning of this?

Phe. We have told your uncle of your unexpected arrival, Mr. Frank Hardy.

Harry. (*Aside.*) Oho! my uncle; gad, then I'll soon make myself one of the family.
(*Shakes hands very heartily with Hardy.*)

Har. But let me look at you, you rogue; I have not seen you since you were a mere urchin. As Phebe says, he is a pretty little fellow. But I say, Frank, you don't take after the family. Your father was a tall man: all tall men in our family.

Harry. Why, I am not positively a giant, uncle; but what does that signify? Nelson was a little fellow like myself—so, not an inch taller will I grow.

Har. Ah, ah, you are a wag. But tell me, Frank, when you found yourself pursued and in danger of a drubbing from my servants, why didn't you at once discover yourself to be my nephew.

Harry. Eh—to say the truth, that never once occurred to me.

Har. Well, your secret was in good hands with the girls. I was in a thundering passion to be sure—your poor cousin has scarcely yet recovered from her agitation.

Harry. Ah, sir, I know not how I shall atone to my cousin for the embarrassment my thoughtlessness has occasioned her.

Eli. I'll never, never forgive you.

Har. What's that I hear? when I have forgiven his wild sailor prank, how dare anybody—go, Frank, give your cousin a kiss, or I'll storm the house about your ears.

Harry. Not through any disobedience of mine, uncle. (*Crosses and kisses Eliza.*)

Eli. Ha' done, Mr. Stan—ha' done, cousin, that will do, (*aside*) I'm glad he is obedient to pa, though.

Phe. (*Wiping her lips.*) My master is right, since he is satisfied, there is no reason why anyone else should be angry.

Harry. And you, too, my pretty Phebe: your lips are as full of forgiveness as mine are of repentance, I'll answer for it.
(*Kisses Phebe.*)

Har. (*Coming down*, R.) Come, come, Frank, you are forgiven. (*Aside.*) I must look close after the young dog, or I foresee we shall have him asking pardon of all the maids in the house. Now, Frank (*Frank crosses to Hardy.*) I have news for you. Eliza is soon to be married,

Harry. Married, sir?

Har. Married, ay, married. I was resolved to defer the ceremony till your return. So now you are here——

Harry. That was very kind; and whenever Eliza marries, you may be sure I will be at the wedding. And pray, sir, who is the happy man?

Har. What is that to you? I know, and that is sufficient for all parties.

Harry. Certainly, sir! but pray does my cousin love him?

Har. No, but she may if she likes. I'm not one of those tyrannical fathers who would control the affections of their children. No, no, I leave my daughter sole mistress of her inclinations; free either to love her husband, or to leave it alone, as she thinks best.

Harry. How indulgent a parent! Now, suppose, sir, I should object to your arrangement?

Har. You object, you jackanapes! Harkee, it is rather the soonest for you and I to quarrel—now, that we may remain friends, you will please to recollect, that although I am willing to listen to reason, argument, and advice, it must proceed from those who have the good sense to be exactly of my way of thinking. But, if anyone dare contradict or oppose me, I!—no, I am not like my poor friend Witherton, but am lord and master in my own family.

Harry. (*To Eliza.*) Then our only hope is the yellow post-chaise.

Har. But come. (*Crossing to* L.) Frank, your flying leaps must have given you an appetite; so follow me and take a snack.

[*Exit Hardy,* R.

Harry. I'll follow you, sir. My dear Phebe, what could induce you to risk such an imposition upon the Colonel? We cannot long escape detection.

Phe. As you said, sir, when you came in at the window, "Any port in a storm." And such a storm as we should have had if you had been abruptly discovered in your own character——

Harry. Well, here I am installed as your cousin; it will be very pleasant as long as it lasts; but I fear we shall pay dearly for it in the end.

Eli. I tremble to think of the consequences. Harry, what colour did you say Mr. Doubledot's post-chaise was?

Harry. The prettiest runaway colour imaginable —will you go and look at it?

Phe. Nonsense, nonsense, we must do nothing rash. Your cousin, the real Mr. Frank Hardy, will not be here for a week, so we have plenty of time for consideration. Why, I declare, here is Mr. Pry again!

PAUL PRY *appears at the door,* L.

Pry. There he is. A most extraordinary circumstance. (*Aside.*) The letter is a good excuse for my return.

Eli. Why he is making signs at me.

Harry. The devil he is; he shall answer that to me. What do you want, sir?
(*Brings down Pry between himself and Eliza.*)

Pry. Nothing.

Harry. Lookye, Mr. Scout. I owe you a round dozen for sailing in chase of me this morning; now explain the signals you were hanging out to my own dear little—to my cousin, Miss Hardy—or—

Pry. Your cousin? So then you are the nephew from sea, after all. My dear sir, you are welcome to England.

Harry. Come, sir, no evasion; explain—or overboard you go.
(*Pointing to the window.*)

Pry. Holloa! well, this comes of doing a civil thing.

Harry. Come, come, sir, be quick, or you'll find me as good as my word.

Pry. There. then, since you will have it. (*Gives Eliza a letter.*) I intended to give it to you mysteriously; but hang me if ever I do a good-natured thing again.

Eli. (*Looking at it.*) There is no need of mystery, sir. (*To Harry.*) It is from my cousin Frank, but ——how came this letter in your possession? It ought to have been delivered by the postman.

Pry. No matter—I am always in the wrong.

Phe. But how came you by it at all?

Pry. Because I am a good-natured fool, and do all I can to oblige. I met the postman the other day, and as I always make it a rule to inquire who has letters, I found that there was one for you (*to Eliza*); and I said that as I was coming past the door, I'd leave it for him, it was the only one he had for the house; poor fellow! you know those postmen have really a long way to walk now, and I thought it would be but civil if I brought it to you.

Phe. Where the deuce was the civility of your doing what the postman must have done?

Pry. Where? why he had his rounds to go: so that Miss Eliza would have had her letter five minutes earlier than by waiting for him, if it had not slipped my memory for a week.

Eli. Why, it is a week old.

Pry. That is because I promiscuously forgot it.
(*Goes up.*)

Eli. (*Who has been reading the letter.*) Heavens! it is all over with us, Phebe; my cousin Frank will really be here to-day. This letter was to apprise us of his arrival a week sooner than we expected.

Phe. There! now is our only hope, which was in leisure for deliberation, destroyed—and through his interference again.

Enter SIMON, L.

Sim. (*To Harry.*) My master waits for you, sir, and is growing impatient.

Har. I'll come. Let us go to the Colonel. I'll devise some excuse for leaving him—intercept Frank on his way hither—enlist him in our cause—and then throw ourselves on your father's mercy.

Phe. I wish you joy of his mercy when he discovers the trick we have played him.

Eli. Mr. Pry, if you did but know——

Phe. (*Interrupting her.*) Nothing.—Simon, Mr. Pry is waiting till you open to door for him again.

Har. And Mr. Pry may consider himself fortunate—(*pointing to the window*)—that I have not spared you that trouble, Simon.

[*Exeunt Harry, Eliza, and Phebe,* L.

Pry. Well, I have done my utmost to serve this worthy family; and all I have gained by it is——

So, Simon, the young spark turns out to be your master's nephew, after all.

Sim. (*Pointing off.*) Now, sir, if you please.

Pry. He intends that as a hint, I suppose. Well, that letter appeared to perplex them. I shan't be able to rest till I have come to the rights of it. Ecod! I'll go down to Doubledot's, and just inquire whether he happens to know anything about it.

[*Exit Simon and Pry.*] L.

END OF ACT II.

———

ACT III.

SCENE I.—*A Room at Doubledot's.*

PAUL PRY *discovered at the table in* c. *with a newspaper; he examines the books and slate in the drawer in table.*

Pry. Well, Doubledot does not return. Out, out, from morning till night. What can he have to do out? No wonder the Green Dragon carries all before it—but if men won't attend to their business—(*Counts a score.*) Two and twenty. Upon my life, it is very discreditable to run such a score at a public-house—who can it be? marked with an S—s. I'll lay my life it is Mrs. Sims—that woman owes money at every shop in the village.

Dou. (*Speaks without,* L.) This way, sir, if you please.

Pry. Oh, at last. A traveller with him—I wonder who he is.

Enter DOUBLEDOT and FRANK HARDY, L.

Dou. (*Very obsequiously at first, but gradually relaxing in his civility.*) This way, sir,—will you please to take anything after your journey?

Fra. No, nothing.

Dou. Will you order your dinner now, sir?

Fra. I shall not dine here. Let my luggage be brought into the house, and remain here for the present. (*Sits* R. *of table.*)

Dou. Ah! a precious customer. (*Aside.*) A glass of water and a tooth-pick.

Pry. I say, Doubledot—a good quantity of luggage for one person! He is alone? Do you happen to know who he is?

Dou. No—but you very soon will, I'll answer for it.

[*Exit,* L.

Fra. Now to proceed to my good old uncle's. After an absence of so many years, I shall scarcely be recognised by him. As for Eliza, who was a mere child at the period of my departure——

Pry. (*Who has seated himself* L. *of table and taken up a newspaper.*) Pleasant journey, sir?

Fra. Very pleasant, sir.

Pry. From London, sir?

Fra. No, sir.

Pry. O, not from London. Stay long in these parts, sir?

Fra. Quite uncertain, sir. A tolerable inquisitive fellow this.

Pry. Shy—don't like him—something mysterious about him. I am determined to find out who he is. Beg pardon, sir, if I'm not mistaken your name is—a——?

Fra. You are right, sir, Snooks. Now, sir, allow me to ask you a question. Is it far hence to Colonel Hardy's?

Pry. Oh, you know him! do you happen to know his nephew, who has just come home from sea?

Fra. Come—coming you mean.

Pry. Come, I tell you. He arrived this morning.

Fra. What, his nephew, Frank Hardy?

Pry. The same. I saw him with my own eyes. Come in a very odd way, too. (*Aside.*) The intelligence appears to perplex him.

Fra. (*Aside.*) What can this mean? (*Rising, and crossing to* L.) A person there assuming my name! doubtless some piece of roguery is intended, which my timely arrival may prevent. I'll find some favourable pretence for visiting the family as a stranger, and observe what is going forward before I declare myself.

Pry. (*Aside.*) An adventurer.

Fra. The Colonel, I believe, sir, enjoys a reputation for hospitality. Do you imagine he would refuse the visit of a stranger?—a gentleman travelling for his pleasure, who wishes to be favoured with a view of his grounds—his pictures.

Pry. (*Hesitating.*) No, sir. (*Aside.*) A travelling gentleman—the case is clear.

Fra. There is no time to be lost, sir. I must be plain with you. It is my intention to pay Colonel Hardy a visit, the object of that visit is important, and that it may succeed the utmost secrecy and caution are requisite.

Pry. Indeed. (*Aside.*) Very cool, upon my word.

Fra. To use your own expression, "Beg pardon if I am mistaken" (*crossing to* L., *and shaking his cane at Pry*) but you appear to me to be one of those good-natured, inquisitive, officious persons, who abound in such places as this. Now if you mention to any soul breathing that you have seen me, you may have cause to repent your indiscretion.

[*Exit,* L.

Pry. Sir, yours. Not the shadow of a doubt what sort of gentleman he is. Yet he looks like a gentleman, but what of that? every pick-pocket now-a-days is described as a youth of prepossessing appearance, and every disorderly woman taken before a magistrate is sure to be young and interesting. Now, what ought I to do in this case? I hate to interfere with other people's business. Yet, in a matter like this—I'll take a short cut to the house, be beforehand with the travelling gentleman, put the Colonel on his guard, and for once force him to acknowledge the value of my service.

[*Exit,* R.

SCENE II.—*At Hardy's—same as in Act II.*

Enter HARDY, MARIAN, and WILLIS, R.

Har. What! marry his housekeeper, marry Mother Subtle! The old fool! The old dotard! Oh, that I were his father for one quarter of an hour, that I might enjoy the paternal gratification of breaking every bone in his body.

Wil. Fortunately the evil is not yet accomplished, and your interference may prevent it.

Har. But how did you learn this?

Wil. My suspicions long existing of such an intention, were confirmed by a desperate altercation between Grasp and Mrs. Subtle, which I have just had the good fortune to overhear. Grasp having detected her schemes upon my uncle, threatened, even at the peril of his own ruin, to expose the intrigues she had so long carried on against me. Mrs. Subtle, presuming on her strong influence over Mr. Witherton, scoffed at his menaces, dared him to do his worst, and defied him to the proof of his accusation, till Grasp hinted at certain letters which unknown to her he had preserved, she instantly moderated her haughty tone, promised compliance with any arrangement he might propose, and once more, I believe, they are friends.

Har. Friends! accomplices you mean. But let me see, what's to be done? First do you return, both of you, and——

Mar. I wish that could be avoided. Mrs. Subtle already assumes the mistress, and has expressed her determination to dismiss me, and——

Har. That will do. You take her at her word. You shall remain concealed here for awhile; egad, and so shall you, Somers.

Wil. To what purpose, sir?

Har. Leave it to me. 'Tis here—'tis here. (*Striking his forehead.*) Go in my study; there you will be free from observation; no one dares go there without my leave. I'll come to you presently, and dictate a letter you shall send to Witherton, which if it does not bring him to his senses he is incorrigible.

Wil. How shall we thank you for the interest you take in our behalf?

Har. By leaving me to myself a few minutes. I have my hands full of business already. Here is a letter I have just received from an old friend, relative to a runaway son of his! Then there's my nephew, Frank, who has returned. But go—go; if my daughter, or her chattering maid, should see you here together, I would not give you five minutes' purchase for your secret.

Mar. We will act implicitly by your advice, sir.

Har. Do so, and I will yet blow all Mrs. Subtle's schemes—no matter where. (*Exeunt Marian and Willis, L.*) Now just let me look at old Stanley's letter again, before I communicate its contents to my nephew. (*Reads.*) "My boy Harry, who is a hare-brained, harem-scarem fellow, mounted horse, and galloped away, the moment I mentioned a wife for him of my choosing. He has been met on the road towards your place, and I suspect that he has discovered who the girl is, and has a mind to see her before he positively rejects her. Should this be the case, detain him till my arrival, which will speedily follow your receipt of this." Ah, this is very pretty, but what right has any man to come and look at my daughter: to take her, or leave her, as he would a horse. My Lizzy is a wife for an emperor; I know it, that's enough, and I won't allow any man to—(*calls out of window.*) Here, you Frank, I want you.

Harry. (*Within, L.*) Coming, sir.

Har. Coming, sir; then why the devil don't you come. There he is, tied to the woman's apron-strings. Hang me, if I have been able to keep him with me during three consecutive quarters of a minute since here he has been.

Enter HARRY STANLEY, ELIZA and PHEBE hanging on each arm, L.

Harry. Did you call me, sir?

Har. Yes; but I didn't call all three of you. Yet here you go about with your heads together, like three conspirators, as if you were hatching another gunpowder treason.

Harry. Can you be surprised at my preferring the company of my dear little cousin to yours, sir? But what have you to say to me, sir?
                              (*Crosses to Hardy.*)

Har. Something that touches the honour of us all. Yours, yours, and (*to Phebe*) even yours, if you have any respect for your mistress.

Harry. (*Aside.*) Am I discovered?

Har. (R.) I have reason to believe that a certain person is in this neighbourhood, cruising under false colours, as you would call it.

Harry. (R. C.) Ah, sir, then I suppose you expect that he should face to the right-about, and beat a retreat, as you would call it.

Har. No, you jackanapes, I neither expect nor intend any such thing. I intend to humour the deception, and then take him by surprise.

Phe. (*Aside, C.*) You have but one chance for it, sir, confess at once—confess.

Harry. Our only hope, I believe. Then what if he should confess his error, ask pardon for his indiscretion, and throw himself upon your mercy?

Har. Why, then I should say, take my daughter, and may you be happy together.

Harry. Would you, sir, why then——
            (*Taking Eliza by the hand and turning towards him.*)

Har. But not so fast. You don't know your uncle yet, Frank. I'll first punish him for his impertinence? How dare he, when it is settled that he shall marry my Lizzy, presume to have a choice of his own? and because he has not yet seen her, how dare he——

Eli. Not yet seen me? Who are you talking about, pa?

Harry. Your intended husband, to be sure, Mr.——

Enter SIMON, L.

Sim. Mr. Paul Pry sends his compliments, and wishes to see you on most important business.

Har. Confound Mr. Paul Pry! Eternally that Mr. Paul Pry. My compliments, and I am not at home. (*Exit Simon, L.*) I guess what his important business is likely to be. He comes to look for a shoestring, or tell me some nonsensical event that has occurred in the neighbourhood.

Pry. (*Without.*) Pooh, pooh! this is no time for ceremony, so see him I must.

Enter PAUL PRY, C. doors.

Pry. Colonel, you must pardon the intrusion, but I come to tell you——

Har. Well, be quick. What cat in the village has kittened? How many blind puppies have your neighbours drowned? Come, inflict upon me the full and true particulars, and make an end of it.

Pry. Colonel, I don't understand. There is treason and a plot in the wind, and I came, like a good-natured fool as I am, to put you on your guard. But there is no time to spare. He is now on his way hither.

Har. He! and who is *he?* and what is *he?*

Pry. An impostor—an adventurer—or something of that mysterious nature. A travelling gentleman, as he calls himself. He has just arrived, and luckily for you I have wormed his intentions out of him.

Har. Well, well, and what are his intentions?

Pry. To get into your house under pretence of seeing your pictures—looking at your grounds——

Har. (*Aside.*) That's my man. Well, and what is there so extraordinary in that?

Pry. Oh, nothing. But when a man talks about the object of his visit requiring the utmost secrecy and caution—when he asks suspicions questions—

Har. What do you call suspicious questions?

Pry. First, he asked me whether you were of a hospitable turn, which I take to be very suspicious. If you had but seen him when I told him of the arrival of your nephew, Mr. Frank, he staggered—absolutely staggered. "What, his nephew?" says he, "Frank Hardy?"

Eli. (*To Stanley.*) Surely this must be my cousin Frank.

Harry. I'll away and prepare him.

Phe. No, leave that to me. My absence will not be remarked.

[*Exit, L.*

Har. Pray, did he mention his name?

Pry. Name! bless you, these fellows have a name for every town in the kingdom. He calls himself Snooks—but, lord bless you——

Har. (*Aside.*) The cautious rogue. But I'll be even with him. No, no, it isn't my pictures he comes to see.

Pry. You may well say that. (*Aside.*) This time, however, he will acknowledge his obligations to me.

Harry. Now, Mr. Pry, it is proper I should tell you that I was already prepared for this visit. I know who the person is, and have most serious reasons for humouring his frolic. I know you to be a busy, meddling, talkative person, and therefore warn you, that if you breathe a hint of having put me on my guard, as you call it—you know me, so I need say no more.

Pry. Well, between the two—Colonel Hardy, you are a magistrate and I—I haven't a shilling about me, or I'd make oath in your presence never to do a good-natured thing again whilst I live.

[*Exit, L.*

Harry. If I could but see him. (*Aside.*) Hadn't I better go and inquire into the truth of this, sir? That blundering booby confuses everything.

Har. No, sir, you will please stay where you are. (*Crossing to Eliza.*) This is he, my love—this Mr. Snooks, as he calls himself, is the person you are to marry.

Eli. Oh, papa, and would you have me marry a man with such a name? I could not if he were a lord.

Har. No, my dear, no—that is not his name. I may tell you now—his name is—no, I won't;—his project in this incognito, and mine in humouring it, might both be defeated by your inadvertently naming him—so 'tis safer as it is. (*To himself*) But I forgot my prisoners. Frank, I have business that will occupy me for a few minutes in my study. Should this gentleman arrive before my return, you, as my nephew, will do the honours for me; and you, my little darling, will remember, that as he is your intended husband, you must endeavour—but I need say no more; that hint is always sufficient to put a woman to her sweetest looks and best behaviour.

[*Exit, R.*

Harry. I am in a pleasant dilemma here. Should this be Frank, I must cease to act your cousin. Should it be the person your father expects, good-bye to my hopes of becoming your husband.

Enter PHEBE.

Phe. Where is the Colonel?

Harry. In his study.

Phe. 'Tis Mr. Frank himself. But be not alarmed, I have prepared him by a hasty narrative of the events of the morning, and he has promised to make one of our party. You may come in, sir.

Enter FRANK HARDY, L.

Fra. My dear cousin! (*Embraces Eliza.*) What, Harry, my old shipmate?

Eli. And is this my little cousin Frank? How much he has grown since he was a little boy!

Fra. We are both somewhat changed. I left home a boy, and returned a man. I left you playing with a doll, and find you manœuvring for a husband. This pretty maid has informed me of your proceedings. But pray, my dear fellow, does it occur to you that we are in a devil of a scrape here?

Har. And pray, my dear fellow, does it occur to you how I am to get out of it?

Fra. (*Pointing to the window.*) That seems the shortest way.

Har. That led me into it, and I never take the same road twice.

Fra. But since my uncle doesn't expect two nephews, one of us must abdicate.

Phe. I hope you didn't come all the way from the antipodes to tell us that, sir. That must be the end of it, we know; but if you were at all acquainted with your uncle's character, you would conceive that there might be some danger in an abrupt disclosure of the deception we have been forced to put upon him.

Fra. How forced?

Phe. Why, as I told you by the way, sir, to prevent lord knows what mischief.

Fra. Harkye, you and I are old friends : you love my cousin, she loves you ; and if my assistance is likely to promote your union, you may command it. Would your father consent to it?

Har. I doubt that, for he has a scheme of his own for my marriage. So my notion is to marry first and ask his consent afterwards.

Eli. Stop, I have an idea.

Phe. (*Aside.*) At last! if it be really an idea, she never came honestly by it—(*Noise without.*) Hush! I tremble at every sound. I'll go and see what it is.

[*Exit, C.*

Har. Now for your idea.

Eli. I dread my pa's anger and dare not see him till he is pacified. Now if Harry were to force me to run away with him whilst you——

Fra. This is a step I will not sanction. Be prudent or I abandon you. But pray tell me, since I am not to be myself, who am I?

Har. Why the Colonel expects his *protégé*. He believes you are the person and——

Fra. That will never do, for should he really arrive, our difficulty would be increased.

Har. There's no time for deliberation, for here comes your uncle.

Fra. (*Aside.*) I long to throw myself into his arms, yet dare not.

(*They retire up.*)

Enter HARDY, R.

Har. We have dispatched the letter, and if that fail to arouse old Witherton to a sense of his humiliation,——(*Aside.*) Ha, there he is. Now I'll teach him to come here and take my whole family as it were upon trial. I believe I have the honour of addressing the travelling gentleman who has expressed a desire to see my pictures.

Fra. (R. C.) Sir—I——

Har. Sir, I entreat you will use no ceremony—visit my grounds—examine my furniture—settle your opinion upon everything and everybody in my house. This is my daughter. (*Takes her by the hand.*) My daughter, sir, you understand. I hope you like her. This is my nephew, Frank. What is your opinion of him? I'm his uncle!—how d'ye like me?

Fra. So well, sir, that if I were to choose an uncle for myself, you would be the very man.

Har. Well, that's one point in our favour. But we have not done yet—my dinners—my wines—it is important that those should be to your satisfaction, young gentleman?—so I shall request the satisfaction of your company at dinner to-day.

Fra. Ay, sir, and to-morrow, and every day for a month to come, if you please.

Har. And if anything in my house dead or alive should displease you, you understand—pray use no ceremony in mentioning it.

Fra. What the deuce does he mean? Sir, I assure you everything here is perfectly to my taste.

Har. If not, Mr. Snooks has but to gallop to town again, and no party—you understand, is compromised by his visits.

Fra. Upon my soul, sir, I do not understand—Snooks?—oh, I perceive; the chattering fellow I met at the inn, has spoken to you about me, and be hanged to him.

Har. No matter, sir, I am very proud of the honour you intend me, and let that suffice.

Harry. (*Aside to Frank.*) Don't contradict him or he'll talk for a month.

Har. And now, sir, that no time may be lost, suppose you commence your inspection at once by a ramble about my grounds. If you please my daughter shall accompany you: but if that is the least disagreeable, pray say so.

Harry. (*Taking her arm.*) Come, and thank heaven for this respite.

Har. What the deuce, Frank—(*Separates them.*) Do the civil thing to the travelling gentleman. Will it be in any way disagreeable to you, sir, to give my daughter your arm?

Fra. Let this attest that it is the most agreeable thing you could have proposed to me, sir.

Har. (*Aside.*) I am sorry it is so. I almost wish he had disliked her, that his marriage might have been a punishment to him for presuming to have a choice of his own. But his father will soon be here—and then——

Enter PHEBE, L., *with a key.*

Well what is the matter with you?—what has alarmed you? Is the house on fire? Why don't you answer?

Phe. Alarmed! no, sir! I am not alarmed; but Grasp, Mr. Witherton's steward, wishes to see you —and running to tell you has taken my breath away, that's all, sir.

Har. So the letter has produced its effect, I imagine.

Phe. He seems in a violent rage, so pray go to him, sir, go.

Har. Well, why need you be so alarmed about it? But you have nerves, I suppose. Ah, the luxury and refinement of the times! Here's a chambermaid sent into the world with as fine a set of nerves

as a duchess. I'll go to the man. You'll excuse me for a short time, Mr. travelling gentleman; Frank and my daughter will supply my place.

[*Exit,* L.

Eli. Phebe, what are you so flurried about? Is it really Mr. Grasp, or have you deceived my pa?

Phe. No, miss, no; that's true enough—but I wish it were the whole truth. He's come at last, and I have him under lock and key.

Eli. Who, the young man?

Phe. Young! why, miss, he's fifty.

Harry. You have mistaken the person then; 'tis a young man the Colonel expects.

Phe. The Colonel speaks of him as he was, without considering how many years have passed since. I am certain 'tis he, for he asked to see the bride—that was enough for me. I thrust him into the breakfast parlour, and locked the door. Here, take the key, and settle your matters as best you may.

Harry. They'll be easily settled. (*Takes the key.*) I have but one way of treating with a rival. Come with me, Frank.

Fra. Hold! Harry, stay where you are. You are too deeply interested in the issue to be as cool as circumstances may require, so leave the interview entirely to me. Come, Phebe, and show me to the dragon I am to vanquish.

Eli. And tell him, Frank, that I can never love him—that we shall never be happy together—and that though I may be obliged to marry him to please my pa, I shall never do anything to please him.

[*Exeunt Harry and Eliza,* R., *Frank,* L.

SCENE III.—*A Landscape.*

Enter MRS. SUBTLE *with a bundle of papers.*

Mrs. S. I have secured them—the arch-villain! (*Looks at the papers.*) The suppressed letters of Witherton and Somers, which he has so often assured me were destroyed, he has artfully preserved. Possessing these, he might indeed have worked my ruin. Now let him expose my practices to Hardy; let him endeavour to traduce me to his drivelling master—these in my power, I fear him not. In my sway over the old man's affections lies my security! Be the accusations of Grasp, therefore, vehement as they may, unsupported by these, the only proofs against me, my simple word shall outweigh them. But how shall I excuse the departure of Marian and Willis? and at such a moment, 'tis unfortunate! The old man is strongly attached to them, and—no matter—I will find means to excuse that to him. These were what most I had to fear; they are mine, and now to destroy these papers (*as she is about to tear them*). Ha! some one comes this way.

[*Exit,* L.

Enter PAUL PRY, *with a fishing-rod.*

Pry. (*Looks at his watch*) Bless me! I thought it was later. If Pope Gregory, when he took upon himself to regulate the years, had hit upon some scheme for shortening the days, he would have conferred an eternal obligation upon us gentlemen who have nothing to do. The days are a deal too long, and positively there is no getting pleasantly through them. Well, I'll go and fish. I expected that Hardy would have invited me to dinner, and from what I saw going forward in the kitchen—the curmudgeon—hang the rod!

[*Exit,* R.

Enter FRANK HARDY, OLD STANLEY, *and* PHEBE.

Phe. Here, outside the enemy's walls, we may confer securely.

Fra. (*Seeing Pry*) What! this man again?

Pry. Ah, ah! how dy'e do? A friend of yours, eh! (*Bows*) Well, you have been to Hardy's?

Fra. I have, and find that, notwithstanding the caution I gave you, you have divulged my intentions. You may recollect the promise I made you? Now, sir——

Pry. Sir, I beg you will excuse me. I'm going to fish. I wish you good day. Isn't that Mrs. Subtle yonder? To be sure it is; what is it she is doing there. Gad, there it goes. Now the loss of that may be the ruin of the poor woman. I'll run after her and see what I can do to help her.

[*Exit Pry.*

Fra. So, sir, I believe we understand each other. You consent to relinquish your share in the treaty with the Colonel respecting his daughter's marriage.

Old S. A marriage with his daughter would have served to strengthen an old friendship; but since the happiness of two persons must have been sacrificed, upon that consideration——

Fra. Sir, you prove at once the goodness of your heart and the soundness of your understanding.

Old S. Is Hardy aware of your affection for his daughter?

Fra. No; and sure if he were, he would not listen to my proposals so long as his engagement with you subsists.

Phe. Now, sir, let me recommend that instead of seeing the Colonel as you proposed, you write to decline the continuance of the treaty. Entrust us with the letter, and I'll answer for the result, which shall be agreeable to all parties.

Old S. My Harry has never seen the girl. She loves another, and it shall be so. Since it is agreed that I am not to have an interview just now with my old friend, and to say the truth the violence of his temper would render it rather an unpleasant one under our present circumstances, pray be so good as to step with me to the inn hard by, and there I will prepare the letter for you. I believe you told me that the Colonel's nephew, and the favoured lovers, are the only visitors at the house.

Fra. Exactly so, sir.

Old S. Plague take the boy, where can he be gone? It's certain he is not here.

Fra. Now, sir, I am at your service. (*Aside*) This engagement relinquished, my friend Harry's suit will be the more readily granted.

[*Exeunt* R.

Phe. Well, when I marry I'll not leave the choice of a partner to the Colonel. The man would be well enough for a grandfather, but for a husband—Miss Simpleton has catered much better for herself. Her Harry is a dashing little fellow, that's the truth on't. The song he sung to us was pretty enough; egad! as I've nothing else to do, I'll try to remember it.

SONG—"Cherry Ripe."

Cherry ripe, cherry ripe, ripe, I cry;
Full and fair ones; come and buy;
If so be you ask me where
They do grow, I answer there;
Where my Julia's lips do smile,
There's the land of cherry-isle.
        Cherry ripe, cherry ripe, &c.

Cherry ripe, cherry ripe, ripe, I cry;
Full and fair ones; come and buy;
Where my Julia's lips do smile,
There's the land of cherry-isle;
There plantations fully show,
All the year where cherries grow.
        Cherry ripe, cherry ripe, &c.

[*Exit,* R.

SCENE IV.—*Drawing Room at Witherton's.*

Enter WITHERTON, R.

Wit. Marry! at the very sound I feel myself a happy and contented man. Marry! and yet at my age 'tis a step which ought not to be inconsiderately taken. Were I to consult with Hardy he would but laugh at me. Willis. (*Rings.*) His advice has served me on more than one occasion. Ah, had my nephew been where he ought, I had not needed the friendship of a stranger; but that young man shall supply his place.

Enter SERVANT, *with a letter,* L.

Desire Mr. Willis to come to me.

Ser. Mr. Willis is gone, sir—and here is a letter for you, sir.

[*Exit,* L.

Wit. Gone! what does he mean? (*Opens the letter.*) What do I read? "Mrs. Subtle's tyranny—her overbearing insolence—unable any longer to endure it—by at once quitting your house, and relinquishing your protection, and 'tis with unfeigned sorrow and regret I do so, I am but anticipating my intended dismissal. Willis, for reasons which you shall know hereafter, has resolved to accompany me.—Marian." My poor Marian! Driven from my house—Willis, too? Does she already so presume? I see my conduct now must determine the character I am to maintain hereafter. I must teach her that I can be master, or I sink for ever into the abject slave.

Enter MRS. SUBTLE, L.

Mrs. S. The papers are destroyed—and now—

Wit. So, Mrs. Subtle, where is Marian? where is Willis?

Mrs. S. Gone!

Wit. By whose authority are they dismissed? Yours?

Mrs. S. Why, how is this? Rebellion? (*Aside*)

Wit. Have you done this, I say?

Mrs. S. No—and if I had, give me leave to say, sir——

Wit. I perceive your error: let me correct it while there is yet time. He that has occasionally endured the control of a servant, may yet revolt at the dominion of a wife. Remember, besides, you assume the mistress somewhat prematurely. Let Willis and Marian be recalled.

Mrs. S. Is it possible? (*Aside*) I know not where they are, sir.

Wit. Restore them to my house, or——

Mrs. S. Or you would have me quit it?

Wit. I said not so.

Mrs. S. (*In tears.*) I deserve this. Oh, woman! would you make a man your tyrant, you need but avow to him that you love. 'Tis clear you wish me gone.

Wit. No, Mrs. Subtle, no—but let them be recalled.

Mrs. S. They shall be sought after. But was this well? Do I deserve this unkindness? Marian is young and handsome; and if her presence here displeased me, could you divine no excusable motive for my displeasure?

Wit. Well, dear Mrs. Suhtle, say no more—I was perhaps too hasty. Ah, here comes Hardy.

Mrs. S. I guess the cause of his visit. Grasp, in his rage at my rejection of him, boldly threatened to invent—I know not what idle charges against me, with a view to injure me in your opinion, and knowing Colonel Hardy to be no friend of mine, he has doubtless endeavoured to enlist him on his side.

Wit. You have nothing to fear—shall I listen to calumnies engendered by jealousy and revenge?

Enter HARDY, L.

Har. So, what is this I hear? You have dismissed Willis—poor Marian too—those whom I recommended to your care.

Wit. Well, well, am I am not master in my own house?

Har. No, there's the master of you and your house too. But I'm aware of your intentions. Marry your housekeeper? How old are you? Are you out of your teens? We'll say nothing about years of discretion.

Wit. (R.) Colonel, this is my house.

Har. (C.) I understand—and when I have performed my errand, I'll leave you to the full enjoyment of it. If you marry, what is to become of your nephew? Though when the settlements are drawn, I daresay Mrs. Subtle will take care the poor fellow shall be amply provided for—(to her) you have always been the friend of poor Somers, you know.

Mrs. S. (Aside) Ah, is he there?

Wit. Provide for him? I'll cut him off with a shilling.

Har. Do what? Do you know the meaning of that trivial, dreadful phrase? Would you carry your resentment beyond the grave? Are you not satisfied to enjoy the pleasure of revenge as long as you live? Surely that is long enough for the best—for the worst of us. When we die, 'tis time our resentment should expire too.

Wit. If you wish to preserve my friendship, sir, you will be silent on the subject of my nephew.

Har. 'Tis to render you worthy of mine that I speak. But this is no time for ceremony? your eyes must be opened. Here, Grasp.

Enter GRASP, L.

You have for years been the dupe of this precious pair—by whom poor Somers has been traduced—his letters—yours suppressed—falsified. This honest gentleman, doubtful of being able to persuade you of the truth of his confession, has taken the surer way of making it to me.

Wit. I was already prepared for something of this nature, but he has deceived you; his motives are not unknown to me.

Mrs. S. Let him speak, sir. What intrigues he may have carried on against your nephew I know not. Whatever he would charge upon me he must prove. His word, under present circumstances, is as nothing.

Har. I would give as little for the fellow's word as you would, who seems to know its great value. So, come, sir, to the proofs you told me of.

Mrs. S. Ay, now, villain!

Gra. Ay, now you shall feel what it is to make a dupe of me.   [*Crosses and Exit, R.*

Har. Now, when your eyes are opened, perhaps you will have no objection to acknowledge that you perceive the light of the sun.

Wit. 'Tis a wicked imposture of his—the petty revenge of disappointed hope.

Mrs. S. Let them proceed, sir.

Re-enter GRASP, R.

Gra. They are stolen—I am robbed. (*To Mrs. Subtle.*) 'Tis you have done this.

Wit. What say you?

Mrs. S. This is too stale a device.

Gra. (*Crosses to Hardy.*) The papers I told you of —'twas but this morning I saw them there—my desk has been opened. You (*to Mrs. Subtle.*), you alone had a motive for doing this.

Wit. The trick is evident. Deliver up your keys, and quit my house.

Har. There can be no objection to that. There will be one rogue the fewer in it. (*To Grasp.*) Do you persist in the truth of the disclosure you made to me?

Gra. It matters not. You see which way the wind blows. 'Tis clear, whatever may happen, I can no longer remain here. (*To Witherton.*) Your blind folly deserves a bitter punishment—marry her.   [*Exit, L.*

Har. (*To Mrs. Subtle.*) Now, I daresay you consider this a triumph; but I have yet——

Mrs. S. Mr. Witherton, what further insult am I to receive at the hands of this gentleman?

Har. Hey-day!

Wit. Colonel Hardy, I beg you will recollect that this lady is to become——

Har. Lady! Well, then, my lady Pickle-and-Preserve, since it must be so.

Wit. Sir, the attempts to disgrace her in my esteem, though I doubt not ingeniously concerted, have failed. It remains with you to determine, by your conduct towards her, whether I am to continue your friend.

Har. My determination is taken. Good morning to you. I had prepared a surprise for you, which would have rendered you a happy man for life. You shall not enjoy it till you know better how to deserve it. Good day.

Enter PAUL PRY, L.

Pry. I hope I don't intrude.

Har. You have just dropped in to wish the young couple joy, I suppose?

Pry. I come to wish Mrs. Subtle joy. You must have been dreadfully alarmed when you discovered your loss.

Mrs. S. (R.) What loss—what?

Pry. I saw you drop them, and called after you, but you didn't hear me.

Mrs. S. What are you speaking of?

Pry. Poor Mrs. Subtle, thought I, if these had been her own, it wouldn't so much have grieved her; but to lose a packet of papers belonging to her master——

Har. Eh, what's that? papers?

Pry. Yes! a packet of papers she let fall into the dry well, up yonder. It took me nearly half an hour to hook them out again, and here they are.

(*Pulling them out of his fishing-basket, and swinging them backwards and forwards at the end of the line.*)

Mrs. S. (*About to seize them.*) They are mine.

Har. (*Taking them.*) By your leave. So, so, this

confirms the truth of Grasp's story. (*Looking at them and giving them one by one to Witherton.*) Will this convince you—or this—or this?

Mrs. S. The schemes I have for years been framing, in a moment destroyed by an officious fool.

Wit. (R.C.) May I believe my eyes? The letter desiring my nephew to hasten to England suppressed. And here—(*reads*)—"Again I write to you, my dear uncle, to implore your consent to my marriage." And here "he entreats permission to see me." What say you to this, Mrs. Subtle?

Mrs. S. I scorn to reply. If you believe me implicated in these intrigues—if you have lost your confidence in my truth and honesty towards you, bid me at once begone. In your solitude, your desolate solitude, you will find leisure to repent your injustice, and——

Wit. Say but you are innocent of any participation in this, and——

Har. Say it! Confound her, she'll say it, and swear it too. But are you so blind as not to perceive the drift of her artful speech? Why need you be desolate? why need you be solitary? It has been her wicked policy to render you so. Recall the friends whom nature has provided for you. If you won't, I will: and if you don't like them—give them over to me.

Wit. What mean you?

Har. To restore an injured nephew to you; and if Somers and his wife have suffered through the calumnies this good lady has heaped upon them, your own judgment has done them right in its true estimate of the virtues of Willis and Marian. Come in.

Enter WILLIS and MARIAN, L.

I hate the parade of sentiment. There they are, so take them at once to your heart. They have nothing to be ashamed of, except having an old fool for an uncle.

(*Willis and Marian throw themselves at Witherton's feet.*)

Wit. No, not there—not there! (*Rises and clasps them in his arms.*) To what vile treachery have I been subjected? Mrs. Subtle, you may perceive that your presence here is no longer desirable.

Mrs. S. Think not I desire to remain:—(*Crosses to L.*)—and if I feel a pang at parting with you, it is at the reflection that a few hours more would have made me the mistress of that fortune, which now—may it carry misery wherever it is bestowed.
[*Exit, L.*

Har. There! If you could entertain the slightest regret at the departure of that good lady, I trust that her farewell speech will serve to extinguish it.

[*Witherton, Willis, and Marian, retire up the stage.*

Pry. 'Tis best for him as it is. He'd have caught a tartar; besides, he can be no chicken. Now what age would you take him to be?

Har. At a random guess—turned twenty. Give me your hand. (*To Witherton.*) I congratulate you on your accession to your senses. I am happy in what I have done here. I feel in good humour with myself and everybody else. Will no one ask a favour, that I may enjoy the pleasure of granting it. Will no one offend me, that I may have the gratification of forgiving him?

Enter FRANK HARDY, L.

Fra. If you are in that mood, sir, I can furnish you with employment.

Har. So, Snooks, it is you. (*To Witherton.*) The son of our old friend Stanley, with whom you and I have cracked many a bottle in our young days. He thinks I don't know him.

Pry. The travelling gentleman.

Har. (*to Frank*) Then you intend to confess who you are, and trust to my mercy? but I knew you from the first. I was apprised of your runaway freak, and was resolved to humour it.

Fra. Pray, sir, read this letter.
(*Gives a letter*)

Har. "Archibald Stanley"—a letter from his father.

Pry. (R.) A pass to the next parish I suppose.

Har. (C.) What the deuce! break off his engagement with me; and has he encouraged you in this?

Fra. (L.) Upon my word, sir, he is a very rational old gentleman, and made no sort of scruple in relinquishing his share in the treaty.

Har. So then it appears that my daughter is not agreeable to you, and your father is mad enough to——

Fra. My father, sir?

Har. Ay, sir, and I consider the conduct of old Mr. Stanley in this affair——

Fra. One word, sir. Is the gentleman I have just seen old Mr. Stanley, the father of Harry Stanley?

Har. Why this is stretching the proverb with a vengeance; and do you pretend that you do not know your own father?

Fra. Ha, ha, ha! So then Harry Stanley is the person who you have all along intended for your son-in-law?

Har. Why, who the devil else do you think it was? But at once declare your intentions, sir. Do you persist in refusing my daughter?

Fra. I do, sir; yet, nevertheless, your own intentions will be fulfilled.

Enter SERVANT, L.

Ser. (*To Witherton.*) Mr. Stanley, sir.

Fra. Ah, ah, I foresee a warm explanation here.

Enter STANLEY, L.

Sta. (*Crosses to Witherton, R. C.*) Ah, my old friend! I have made a fruitless journey down to this place, but I would not return to town without shaking you by the hand. (*Turns.*) What, Hardy! I had resolved not to see you, but since we have met, your hand. Your daughter may be all the happier for the exchange.

Har. (L. C.) So then you countenance your son in his refusal? You allow him to come here, look at my daughter, turn up his cursed impudent nose at her, and coolly march off again.

Sta. (C.) What, and has my Hal been here? What has become of him?

Har. Why, don't you see him before you? Turn about, you dog. (*To Frank.*)

Sta. Ha, ha, ha! He's no son of mine.

Pry. That's very mysterious. He don't know his own son.

Har. Tell me, if that is not your son, pray whose son is he?

Sta. That's more than I can say. All I know about him is that he is the gentleman in whose favour I have just relinquished my boy's claim to your daughter.

Har. So, sir, you have dared to impose upon me, by telling me that——

Fra. (L.) You wrong me, sir. I told you nothing. The error was of your own creating.

Pry. (R.) There, you see, I was right. I put you upon your guard.

Har. Ay, and your putting me on my guard has led to this misunderstanding. But here comes my nephew. I shall leave it to him to revenge this affront.

Enter HARRY STANLEY, ELIZA, and PHEBE, L.

Wit. My dear friend, be temperate.

Harry. For all misunderstanding that has occurred here, sir, I alone am—the devil, my father!

Pry. The devil his father! Well, I thought he did not come of a good family, from the first moment I saw him.

Sta. Come hither, sir, and answer your father.

Har. Listen to your uncle, I say.

Sta. You, his uncle! Why, zounds, are you mad, or do you think I don't know my own son?

Har. There is some confounded roguery in this. If one of these is not your son, and the other an impudent rascal of a lover, what am I to do for a nephew?

Phe. (*Leading Frank to him.*) For want of another take this.

Har. I begin to perceive. So then you were the bird-catcher after all, and were already acquainted with my daughter. And pray, Miss Phebe, how did you dare——

Phe. Why, sir, if hot-headed gentlemen will ask questions with pistols in their hands, what is one to do?

Wit. Come, come, say no more. You have your own way.

Har. True, I have my own way, but not in my own way of having it. Her obedience is not quite so evident in this as I could have desired; however, there—(*Crosses to Harry, passes him over to Eliza, and joins their hands*)—there, you bird-catcher, you. You've caught the goldfinch.

Eli. Thank you, pa, and if ever I marry again, you shall have the choice all your own way.

Harry. I am in no hurry to give your pa opportunity of putting your obedience to a test.

Har. Frank, my boy, you take after the fami and I forgive you on that account.

Phe. I hope, sir, you'll forgive me—if not (*Turns to Witherton.*) I hear, sir, that you ha dismissed your housekeeper, and (*curtesys.*) shou I lose my place in the Colonel's family——

Wit. Ah, my dear, you are too young for housekeeper, and I have abandoned my intentio to marry. Celibacy is an error, which at my age is too late to repair. I have been foolish enoug to live single all my life, but to marry now won be but to exchange a great folly for a greater. this is now my refuge for life.

(*Taking Willis and Marian's hands*)

Har. All you that are single, take warning him, and marry as fast as you can.

Pry. (*To Phebe.*) A broad hint to you and m Miss Phebe.

Phe. Lord help me. You are too inquisitive fo a husband.

Pry. Pooh, pooh! A spirit of inquiry is the grea characteristic of the age we live in.

Har. It is a spirit which now and then leads yo to fish in troubled waters.

Pry. (*Crosses to Hardy*). I flatter myself I hav fished to some purpose to-day though—the paper you know.

Har. So you have; and in consideration of that I will tolerate you for the remainder of it. You shall dine with me.

Pry. You'll tolerate me—no, will you? Well that's very polite, and I accept your invitation.

Har. But if you dare ask a single question, eve what it is o'clock, I'll toss you out of the window.

Pry. I must ask one question more. Ladies an gentlemen, if I am not impertinent, will you, wil you overlook the many faults of Paul Pry?

Disposition of the Characters at the fall of the Curtain.

PRY.	HARDY.
WILLIS. PHEBE.	FRANK. HARRY.
MARIAN. WITHERTON.	ELIZA. STANLEY
R.	L.

Lightning Source UK Ltd.
Milton Keynes UK
25 January 2011

166326UK00004B/66/P